Praise for
Sweet Relief

"This book is like savoring a warm cup of coffee with a friend. Kaitlin speaks straight to the heart of the try-hard life and points you to Christ who did all the work required. Her words will challenge, encourage, and cheer you on as you rest in the freedom of the gospel."
—**Michelle Rabon,** author of *Holy Mess*

"This vibrant storyteller recounts the exhausting journey that millions of women—and also men like my two coendorsers—have felt trapped in. Invest a few hours with Kaitlin Garrison and you may well experience *Sweet Relief* the rest of your life."
—**Brittany Sawrey,** Director of Content, Trueface; author of *Two Roads, Crazy Making,* and *Healing Relationships*
—**Robby Angle,** President, Trueface; author of *The Cure for Groups*
—**Dr. Bruce McNicol,** President Emeritus, Trueface; coauthor of *The Cure*

"It's possible to have just enough of Jesus not to need him. Just enough knowledge, just enough language, just enough of the lifestyle to have the appearance of Christianity without the abundant life God intended. Thankfully, Katilin Garrison won't let us settle. Drawing on stories from her own life and wise biblical insight, Kaitlin is waking us up to the freedom we were created. If you are a lifelong Christian who keeps wondering if there is something more, you will find the answer in these pages."
—**Sharon Hodde Miller,** author of *Nice: Why We Love to Be Liked and How God Calls Us to More*

"The struggle to 'do enough' and 'be enough' for God has been the reality of my life over the years. *Sweet Relief* puts words to this tension we can all face and reveals the one thing we've been missing all along—the love of Jesus! Filled with truth and hope, there is freedom to be found in these pages!"
—**Ruth Schwenk,** coauthor of *Trusting God in All the Things*; Founder of TheBetterMom.com

SWEET RELIEF

Kaitlin Garrison

SWEET RELIEF

*How the Gospel Frees Us
From a Life of Striving*

LEAFWOOD
PUBLISHERS
an imprint of Abilene Christian University Press

SWEET RELIEF
How the Gospel Frees Us from a Life of Striving

an imprint of Abilene Christian University Press

Copyright © 2022 by Kaitlin Garrison

ISBN 978-1-68426-501-5 | LCCN 2022011737

Printed in the United States of America

ALL RIGHTS RESERVED
No part of this publication may be reproduced, stored in a retrieval system, or transmitted in any form by any means—electronic, mechanical, photocopying, recording, or otherwise—without prior written consent.

Scripture quotations, unless otherwise noted, are from the Christian Standard Bible®. Copyright © 2017 by Holman Bible Publishers. Used by permission. Christian Standard Bible®, and CSB® are federally registered trademarks of Holman Bible Publishers.

Scripture quotations marked ESV are taken from the ESV® Bible (The Holy Bible, English Standard Version®). ESV® Text Edition: 2016. Copyright © 2001 by Crossway, a publishing ministry of Good News Publishers. All rights reserved.

Scripture quotations marked NIV are taken from the Holy Bible, New International Version®, NIV®. Copyright © 1973, 1978, 1984, 2011 by Biblica, Inc.™ Used by permission. All rights reserved worldwide.

Scripture quotations marked NLT are taken from the Holy Bible, New Living Translation, copyright © 1996, 2004, 2015 by Tyndale House Foundation. Used by permission of Tyndale House Publishers, Inc., Carol Stream, Illinois 60188. All rights reserved.

Library of Congress Cataloging-in-Publication Data
Names: Garrison, Kaitlin, author.
Title: Sweet relief : how the gospel frees us from a life of striving / Kaitlin Garrison.
Description: Abilene, Texas : Leafwood Publishers, [2022]
Identifiers: LCCN 2022011737 (print) | LCCN 2022011738 (ebook) | ISBN 9781684265015 | ISBN 9781684269068 (kindle edition)
Subjects: LCSH: Perfectionism (Personality trait)—Religious aspects—Christianity. | Grace (Theology)
Classification: LCC BV4597.58.P47 G37 2022 (print) | LCC BV4597.58.P47 (ebook) | DDC 155.2/32—dc23/eng/20220321
LC record available at https://lccn.loc.gov/2022011737
LC ebook record available at https://lccn.loc.gov/2022011738

Cover design by Greg Jackson, ThinkPen Design | Interior text design by Sandy Armstrong, Strong Design

Leafwood Publishers is an imprint of Abilene Christian University Press
ACU Box 29138 | Abilene, Texas 79699

1-877-816-4455 | www.leafwoodpublishers.com

22 23 24 25 26 27 28 / 7 6 5 4 3 2 1

*To the strong, godly women who have richly invested
in my life and mentored me over the years—*

*Laura Kirkpatrick, Bethany Vaccaro,
Amanda Gallagher Duron, Ashlee Weaver,
Cynthia Russell, Rachel Calloway,
Erin Bull, Lisa Leduc—*

*I will never stop being thankful for your leadership,
guidance, and words spoken into my life.*

CONTENTS

Introduction | The Heart of a Striver 11
Chapter One | The Heart of the Father 19
Chapter Two | A Heart That Is Centered 31

PART ONE | THE GOSPEL THAT SETS US FREE

Chapter Three | The Marring 41
Chapter Four | The Mediator 53
Chapter Five | The Mending 65
Chapter Six | The Maturing 75

PART TWO | THE FALSE GOSPELS THAT KEEP US STUCK

Chapter Seven | The DIY Gospel 89
Chapter Eight | The "So That" Gospel 99
Chapter Nine | The Gospel of Grit 111
Chapter Ten | The "You Do You" Gospel 123

PART THREE | WHAT THE GOSPEL FREES US TO

Chapter Eleven | Free to Love and Be Loved 133
Chapter Twelve | Free to Trust 145
Chapter Thirteen | Free to Need 157
Chapter Fourteen | Free to Set Others Free 171
Chapter Fifteen | Free to Come Close 183
Final Thoughts | Free to Run 193

Acknowledgments 197
About the Author 201

Introduction

THE HEART OF A STRIVER

I am not enough.

I don't know if I've ever experienced more freedom than I have in admitting those four words. At first, this confession felt toxic; mostly because I wasn't sure if I was even allowed to say something like that. Yet, at the same time, something inside me felt liberated every time I said it.

Free.

As those four words sank in, I could finally catch my breath and gain some clarity after spending so much time aimlessly running. For years, this idea of "being enough" acted like a distant, desert mirage—an illusion of my imagination that sent me on a wild goose chase for an earthly security I'd never find.

All I'd ever wanted was to be enough. Good enough for people, friends, superiors, my community. I wanted to be enough for my own outrageous standards, and eventually, I found myself trying to be good enough for God. At a young age, I observed from the hurried and hustling world around me that in order to be good enough, I first had to be **good**. A good girl.

And that's exactly who I became.

The Birth of the Need to Please

As a young adolescent, I would categorize myself as a rule-following, Bible-reading, sin-avoiding, people-pleasing, well-mannered church girl. I attended Sunday school every week, memorized the most important verses, and started serving as a student leader in ministry by the time I was thirteen.

As someone who was intrinsically motivated by people's approval, I learned very quickly that if I put on my best behavior, said all the right things, and avoided all the wrong things, I could make people adore me. It was invigorating. At the onset of check marks, scores, and sticker charts, my little brain began to grasp all the tangible benefits of a "work-to-achieve" mentality. I learned from the world I lived in that if I worked hard, behaved correctly, and followed the rules, I could earn the acceptance, applause, and accolades of others—a good sign that I was enough for them. The problem? This mentality worked for me.

I worked hard in school and in my jobs and earned the highest affection of my bosses and teachers. Like clockwork, I used this work-to-achieve mentality to get whatever I wanted. From experience, I concluded that I could earn a place of favor through working hard—and that made my soul feel complete. Each applause was one step closer to catching that mirage.

But then I met Jesus. Even though I'd been taught about him all my life, he introduced himself to me when I was fifteen, and I knew I would never be the same after that encounter. The way he healed my heart captivated me, and I wanted to know him for myself. The more I got to know him, the more I fell in love with him. I was in—I wanted to follow him anywhere. But just as with everyone else in my life, I wanted gold star stickers from him too. It didn't take long for this achievement-based mindset to bleed into my theology and what I thought about God. Somehow, when I heard sermons, the only thing that stood out to me was what I needed to *do* to get close to God and *earn* his favor—just like I had everyone else's. If I could sum up the gospel in my own words at that time it would be "If you do enough for him, you'll be good enough for him." Like an annoying song you can't get out of your head, this phrase became an anthem for my every action. I subconsciously built my faith on phrases like these:

- A great performance will earn God's acceptance.
- More works for God helps work your way to God.
- The more you do, the more he's impressed with you.

The bottom line of my beliefs centered around this idea: *I can be good enough for God.* It became a measurable, achievable goal that sent me sprinting.

So, I built. I worked hard, behaved well, busied myself in ministries, and crafted my identity on all the wonderful things I did for God. Every now and then I'd come up for air and ask, "God? Am I still enough for you? Do you still love me?" This mentality became the rock I stood on; that is, until it became the boulder that broke my back. Working out my salvation and Christian life as if it were all up to me was a ridiculously heavy weight to bear. No matter how much "good" I did, it never felt like enough. It left me feeling completely worthless, panic-stricken, and distant from the God I desperately wanted to please.

One weekend about six years ago, I attended a simulcast conference at my college campus, totally unsuspecting that God might meet me there. We were in the middle of worship and the room erupted in praise as we sang about the love of God washing over us. I closed my eyes and sang this refrain over and over, but my eyes shot open when the Lord impressed these words upon my heart: "You can't receive my love because you are in rebellion against it."

Rebellion? Are you kidding me? In all my striving, that is exactly the thing I sought to avoid. I wasn't a rebel. It wasn't in my blood. In fact, I *loved* following the rules because they benefitted me. So how in the world was God now calling me out for being a rebel?

Over the next couple of months, I earnestly asked the Lord what he meant by those words. He slowly revealed that rebellion is not necessarily an outright insubordination and defiance—it's also a resistance to something. I had resisted and rejected the grace his Son offered me because I whole-heartedly believed I didn't need him.

My life proclaimed this melody: God loves me because I earned it, because I have done enough. In other words, I don't need Jesus because **I am enough.** And this was the very lie that caused me to go blind—to completely overlook God's gifts of grace, salvation through Jesus alone, and the unconditional nature of God's love. This "can't-work-for-it" kind of love and acceptance didn't fit in any of my boxes—it was completely unexpected and foreign. Therefore, in the midst of all my church going, hand raising, gospel sharing, deed doing, and behavior modifying, I had completely lost sight of Jesus. I'd become so busy with godly tasks trying to be enough for Jesus that I slowly eradicated any kind of need for Jesus. Who knew that by hyper focusing on all the right, good, and lovely things that you could become blind and miss the most important thing? In this season, my soul had become a victim to what psychologists refer to as *inattentional blindness*.

Blind and Unaware

Inattentional blindness is a psychological phenomenon in which a person experiences "a surprising failure to notice an unexpected object or event when one's attention is focused on something else."[1] In other words, it is when we miss something that is literally right in front of us because our attention is focused on something we have deemed more important.

In 1999, Psychologists Daniel Simons and Christopher Cabris conducted a study that revealed how people can focus so intently on something that they actually become blind to the unexpected, even if they are staring right at it. They fleshed out this idea of inattentional blindness by creating a video in which a group of people, half wearing black shirts and the other wearing white, passed a basketball back and forth. The video gave an initial task to the viewer to count how many times the ball was passed between the players wearing white shirts.[2] With the viewer's attention fixated on counting the movements of the ball, a shocking 50 percent of viewers completely missed the huge, black gorilla beating his chest who walked right in the middle of them all! I was one of the 50 percent who had succumbed to this inattentional blindness and was convinced someone had rigged this video! (Now that I've ruined the "Invisible Gorilla" video for you, you can go show it to someone and see if they fall for it!)

Like a soul type of inattentional blindness, I became so fixated on godly tasks, managing my behavior, and playing the part that I inadvertently became blind to grace and overlooked his gift of salvation entirely. It was almost like staring at a picture of Jesus yet missing him completely.

When the Lord allowed me to see my rebellion, I felt just about as desperate as a blind man who, in his own strength, cannot make his sight come back. I realized for the first time that this kind of heart change was something I couldn't generate myself. I saw that I needed Jesus because I could not save myself from this. All my life I had known about the sacrifice Jesus made, but this time, I realized I needed it. Brick by brick, the Lord helped me uncover the different distortions of the true gospel I had built around my faith over the years. He renewed my vision and allowed me to see my need for Jesus and the goodness of the real gospel.

My Secret Sin

Maybe you too have found yourself caught in the realization that all these years and after all this time, you've lost sight of him too. Maybe you've been wondering why your life feels filled to the brim with pressure, frequently on the brink of spiritual burnout, and constantly feeling like your relationship with God is hanging in the balance of your good behavior.

I find it interesting that inattentional blindness typically occurs when we are focused on the right things—on the things we are told to look at. The way to catch a person in the pitfall of inattentional blindness is to give them a task that will occupy all their attention, and this will cause them to miss the unexpected thing walking right in front of their eyes. What a sneaky tactic of the enemy.

Sure, maybe the enemy hasn't been able to get you caught up in a cycle of visibly "bad" sin—that would be too obvious to you. Instead, you became busy with a bunch of good things—godly things. In the middle of doing all these wonderful things for God, the enemy began crafting a covert lie, convincing you that God's pleasure with you all this time was merely because of your hard work.

Steadily, through lie after lie, he persuaded you that you could be good enough for God on your own. You could work hard enough and manage your sin in such a way that, subconsciously, your heart believes there is no need for the sacrifice of Jesus because, well, you've done a pretty dang good job on your own.

And that, my friend, is still sin. It's a pride that burrows its way deep into our hearts and typically isn't visible to the outside world. On the inside, it cultivates a heart that inflates from self-righteousness with every good deed, shrivels in shame with every failure, and ultimately stands on the anti-gospel ground of believing our salvation and standing with God are completely dependent on us.

You and I both know this is an incredibly hard place to live. When we live this way, we are blind to the saving gospel of grace. The worst part of all? Our lives display a false gospel to the world.

We don't proclaim that Jesus Christ is the Savior, but rather that we can become our own type of savior. It is never what we intended—in fact, it's the furthest thing from it. Our intentions were to please the God we dearly love. But somewhere along the way, we became so caught up in all the tasks, ministries, and the satisfying work of good deeds that our eyes came unglued from Jesus and fixated on ourselves.

The truth? We are not enough on our own. Our hard work and good merit cannot somehow build a bridge over the chasm our sin created. The good news? Jesus is. He is enough. When we come to know that the all-sufficient one reigns in us, our striving ceases and so does the chase to be good enough. But first, we must realize we need a rescue just like everyone else.

We need the gospel of grace to penetrate our hearts in a fresh way.

When the Lord made my heart aware of my inattentional blindness, I knew I needed to hear the gospel all over again because I had been living the beliefs of a distorted one. And that's exactly what we're going to do through the rest of this book. Together we will rediscover this gospel that eradicates our need to strive and jump through hoops for a God who has already fully accepted us through the perfect blood of his Son. This gospel sets our feet wildly free because we are no longer stuck striving for acceptance but are liberated to run from a place of already being accepted.

If you are sick of an acrobatic, performance-based faith and are thirsting for freedom, hang with me. Let's start off by taking a good, hard look at the heart of the Father for whom we've been working so hard.

Notes

[1] Daniel Simons, "Failures of Awareness: The Case of Inattentional Blindness," in *Noba Textbook Series: Psychology*, ed. R. Biswas-Diener and E. Diener (Champaign, IL: DEF Publishers, 2022). Retrieved from https://nobaproject.com/modules/failures-of-awareness-the-case-of-inattentional-blindness.

[2] Simons, "Failures of Awareness."

Chapter One

THE HEART OF THE FATHER

Extreme confidence is one way to describe my attitude toward my athletic abilities—that is, until my sixth-grade year when I joined the track team. I can vividly remember my inflated pride as I waltzed into my first practice with my pink Nike duffel bag, striped Adidas pants, running shoes, and Icy Hot lathered all over my shins. I was ready to show a bunch of sisters up because, hey, I was really good in fifth grade PE. I was ready to be the best.

Well, let's just say that dream was instantly crushed after day one. After the excruciating warm up, we were tasked with running two miles around the school neighborhood. And where was I? Straggling at the back of the running line, intermittently dry heaving while the rest of the pack waited at the track field for the grannies to make it back.

Practices from this day forward consisted of me graciously taking the back of the line with my track coach following me in his truck. "Pick It UP, Kirkpatrick! Do not let me pass you going 10 mph!" (He was big and burly, but a total softy. I knew he'd never do it.) Eventually, it came time for our second track meet. I had already faked being sick for the first one, so I couldn't use that excuse again. My coach had worked with me all season, and I still wasn't showing a whole lot of progress. Although my coach most definitely didn't expect me to place well, this track meet would be the time to prove him wrong.

Girls from different parts of the state took their place for the one-mile run, and I planted my feet on the inside lane. As soon as the whistle blew, I played through all the advice my coach and my dad had told me. "Go slow and steady." "Don't get caught in the rat race." "Pace yourself."

Well, I paced myself alright.

I was on my fourth lap around the track, and everyone on my team had already finished. It was just me and three other slow pokes from other schools. Surely, I could take them. As I made my last leg around the track, I could see my parents clapping, and I could hear my little brother screaming as loud as he could. But my eye was on my coach's face, staring at his furrowed brow, knowing he was counting on me to not get last place.

In the last one hundred meters of the race, two flying objects with long hair dashed right before my eyes and crossed over the finish line. At that moment, it was as if everything reverted to slow motion. I watched my coach rip his hat off, my teammates throw their heads back, flop their hands down, and let out a very audible, "Nooo!"

Last place.

Gosh, I wanted to hide. In fact, I tried. As soon as I crossed the finish line, I made a beeline straight for my parents and begged them to take me home right then. I did not want to see my coach's face. I didn't want a pity handshake from my teammates. And I certainly did not want to face any of my snickering classmates who were sitting in the stands.

At that moment, I prayed to God that I would just melt into the grass so nobody could see me. Dramatic as it may seem, this was the first time my little heart experienced the biggest side effect of shame—the insatiable need to hide. (Anyone else permanently scarred from middle school?)

Performance-Based Relationships

Up to this point, I hadn't experienced what it was like to repetitively disappoint a coach or person in authority. As previously established—I was a good girl, an achiever, and this was the first time I tangibly felt what it was like to not measure up to someone's standard. Because in my eyes, my coach and I were in what I like to call a performance-based relationship. He gave me the chance to be on his team, and it was my responsibility to give our team a good name and win him trophies. Our relationship was all about exchange.

Now, I know for a fact that no coach I've ever had would say they were in a performance relationship with me. I wasn't a commodity to be used or disposed of; I was a kid to be invested in. Nevertheless, that isn't how I saw them. They were people to be pleased. I watched how they esteemed me, celebrated me in my victories, and how their faces fell in my failure. I concluded that achievement brought acceptance, and failure broke it.

As I encountered more opportunities as a young adult, I unknowingly turned a lot of relationships into performance relationships. They sure didn't know it, but I did. And you know what I found? Intimacy in those relationships fluctuated. Because when I was successful, I gloated in my pride, self-assured that I had done something well, and felt confident enough to come close in fellowship. But when I failed or fell short, I hid and kept my distance.

As I naturally turned loving relationships into performance-driven ones, you can see how easy it became to view my relationship with God as yet another performance-based relationship—but perhaps the most important one. Much like my coach, I felt personally commissioned to make God's team look good and win him trophies.

Being a lifelong church girl, I quickly picked up on Christian lingo, found what was most talked about in sermons and teachings, and concluded that spiritual disciplines and practices were kind of like trophies. When you completed them, God was pleased, and you earned a trophy. So every day, I kept score.

- Quiet time? Trophy.
- Fifteen minutes of prayer? Trophy.
- Memorize Scripture? Gold medal.
- Nice to a rude customer? Trophy.
- Shared the gospel? Two trophies.

Life simply became about doing good things so I would never see God's face fall. I didn't want to see him throw his head back and his arms down. I just wanted his embrace, celebration, and intimacy—and I had established a formula on exactly how to receive that. Therefore, I "worked" my way into his arms and did commendable things so I could stay there. But when I failed, when boxes were left unchecked and I was not good, I didn't want to approach him or come near him because I was caught in a repetitive cycle of shame. Shame is notorious for convincing us to stay at a distance until we feel "worthy" enough to come close.

So I hid until I could come back with a better performance.

With a heart not centered on the saving grace of the gospel, I found myself in a performance-based relationship with my heavenly father, who never intended for intimacy to look this way with his kids. That's the thing about performance relationships: self-satisfaction fuels you to come close, but shame will convince you to pull away and hide. Living this way was exhausting. I was never confident of God's love for me and felt like I was losing it and gaining it back with every failure and every success. Ultimately, my identity was centered around what I could do for God, and not on what God had already done for me. As a performer, my goal was to earn, but the gospel invites us to receive that which we cannot earn. With my hands out straight in resistance, I denied his grace with the confession that I could earn this on my own. But denying God's grace through self-sufficiency just made a running rebel out of me—one who didn't run away by breaking all the rules, but one who ran by trying to keep them all.

The Son Who Stayed Close

In one of Jesus's most popular parables (The Lost Son), he paints this picture of a similar type of performance-based relationship between a father and a son. If you have never heard this story or need a refresher, you can find the story in Luke 15:11–32. In quick summary, a man has two sons. The youngest son approaches the father and asks for his inheritance before the father has died. He essentially says, "You're as good as dead; I want your money." Every parent's dream, right? The father gives the younger son his inheritance only to have it quickly squandered on prostitutes and reckless living. When the younger son has reached the end of his rope, he decides to come back home to the father to work as a servant. But while he was still a long way off, the father sprinted after him, threw his arms around him, and lavished him with meaningful gifts that confirmed his sonship. Then the father threw him a huge party and *almost* everyone came to celebrate. As the party was going on, the older son who was working in the fields heard the music and asked a nearby servant what was going on. The servant informed him that his brother had returned, and his father had invited everyone to come and celebrate his return.

And how did the older brother respond? With fury. He didn't want to be a part of this whole shindig because it wasn't fair. In his anger, the older son refused to go into his father's house. In fact, his father had to leave the party to come and see why the older son wouldn't step foot into his house. After pleading with his son to come in, the older son finally defended his actions to his father by saying things like:

> I've been slaving for you all these years.
> I've never disobeyed your orders.
> You've never done something like this for me.
> But you decided to slaughter the fattened calf for this
> son of yours who blew all your money?
> And you did all this—for *him*? (Luke 15:29–30)

The older son's words reflected the hurt of a broken man who felt betrayed by the father he had worked so hard to please. He was the one who deserved lavish treatment for years of hard obedience and work, not his irresponsible, unthoughtful brother.

Isn't it funny how the people who react the strongest and with the most resistance to grace tend to be those who don't believe they actually need it? Why? Because they've earned the right to good things. Why should people receive goodness without having to bust their tails for it? When you don't think you need grace, you aren't able to give it away. This is the same attitude we see over and over in the lives of the Pharisees, Sadducees, teachers of the Law, and religious leaders who were physically present as Jesus told this parable. Their hearts were hardened to the message of grace Jesus came to deliver.

And the harsh truth is we become exactly like them when we live acrobatic lives, hell-bent on being enough, with a straight arm out to the grace of God. It hardens our hearts in ways we could never imagine and turns us into people we don't even recognize. But I believe Jesus ended the parable the way he did for those who clung to their religion and good merit. He gave clearer resolution about what happened to the wayward son, who had messed up and returned. His father embraced him with love and welcomed him back home. But what about the older son? Did he go back to the father's house? Or did he stay outside, sulking in his bitterness toward the grace his brother had received? We have no idea. Jesus left it open ended.

I think Jesus intended for the story to end this way because it leaves the listener floored by the fact that the rebellious son came and enjoyed a celebration with his father while the "good" son refused to come inside. The Pharisees would have known exactly what this meant. It left them with a choice. It leaves us with a choice.

Tim Keller sums up this scandalous ending quite well in his study guide, "The Two Prodigal Sons":

> Jesus shows us a father with two sons, and actually both are equally alienated from his heart. One has expressed alienation by running far away, but the elder brother is just as angry and is just as much a stranger to the father. The father must *"go out"* to each of them to urge them to come in (v. 20, 28). But here's the remarkable part. One of his sons is a very good person, one is a very wicked person, but in the end, it is the evil son who comes into the Father's feast and dance, and it is the good son who absolutely will not. The listeners knew what that meant. They were utterly stunned. It was a complete reversal of everything they believed. You can almost hear them gasp as the story ended. The lover of prostitutes enters the kingdom of God, and the moral man does not.[1]

A Righteous Rebellion

When I listen to this story, everything in me wishes I had a story like the younger son. Accepting the undeserved grace, repentant and ready to receive. But I don't. I can relate with the self-righteous, moralistic, rule-following tendencies of the older brother who found himself rejecting the invitation of his father at the end of this story.

Because much like the older son, it wasn't my sinful behavior that kept me away from God, it was my own goodness, my enough-ness. To take it a step further, I used my own goodness to, in a sense, control the father—thinking I could use my good deeds to get things from him. But in this story, we see that it was the proximal son, the one who stayed by his father's side the entire time, who was truly wayward at the end of this story.

Rebellion is ultimately telling God, "I don't need you!" And we can demonstrate that rebellion in two ways. Like the younger son, we can try to escape the hand of God through immoral behavior, reckless living, and forsaking wisdom for a sense of freedom. But like the older son, we can escape the love and grace of God because our own goodness convinces us we don't even need it. Friends, this is a scary place to be.

Because we can't behavior-modify or slap a façade on a broken theology. It will eventually make itself known—just like in the older son's life. We cannot generate, muster up, or uproot a deep seeded belief like this by ourselves. We cannot just "know" about this kind of love; we must experience it and receive it. We cannot fix our own unbelief.

We need the Holy Spirit to author change in our hearts that will lead us to acknowledge we are in desperate need of Jesus, repent, and come running to the Savior who can save our souls. Our sweet Savior leaves this story open ended and untold as he stands outside and leaves us with an invitation: "Child, will you come back inside?"

The Return to the Father

Our Father in heaven has a kind heart, and he is crazy about his kids. He is faithful to receive us when we run far from home, and he is gentle to meet us outside his house when we're too prideful to come in. His arms are wide open to receive us with a grace that radically changes and transforms us. There is no love like the love of the Father. His love invites us into something different—it invites us to stop performing for him and to just be his kid. He invites us to believe that he loves us not because of how hard we work for him but because we're his. He made us, designed us, and knows us in a way no human ever could. He longs for us to trust his love, abide in it, and find our new identities in whom he has created us to be.

We will find that being in a relationship with the Father out of love for him creates a new intimacy to know him and be known by him. When we are actively receiving the love of the Father over us, we will find the entire nature of our relationship changes. A performance-based relationship is fueled by guilt, shame, self-righteousness, and control. Therefore, the fruit of that relationship will ultimately be hiding, disillusionment, striving, and distrust. Yet when we receive God's love, come into agreement that we cannot earn it, and abide in the good work that he has already done on our behalf, the fruit of that relationship is assurance, trust in his love, and rest in a new identity centered in Christ's righteousness. It is following what the Father asks because we are sure of his love, know his heart, and trust him deeply. A relationship of trust with the Father is a completely new way to live.

My dear friend, as you consider this invitation today, let me ask you:

- Do you find yourself exhausted from trying to prove yourself to God?
- Are you hiding in shame because of your inconsistency?
- Are you afraid God is disappointed in you?
- Is your relationship with God more about transaction and exchange than love and trust?
- Does your faith feel like a game, winning and losing God's approval of you?
- Do you hold the picture of God smiling in your success and shaking his head in your failure?
- Do you long for security in your relationship with God?

If you answered yes to any of these questions, I want you to know there is good news for you today. There is sweet relief for the soul who has been trying to be her own savior; running on a hamster wheel of trying to earn the acceptance of a God who has already fully accepted her through Christ. But first, we must admit that we need it.

Before we move through the rest of these chapters and take action, I want to invite you into a holy moment. My hope is that from the beginning of this book, we would have a foundation of surrender. That we would take the time to lay down every crown we think we've earned at the feet of the King who has won it all for us. That we would confess our blindness and our inability to make ourselves see. That we would ask our heavenly Father to viciously tear down any "gospel" we've made with our own hands and build our faith on a solid foundation on Jesus alone, which can never be shaken. We cannot perform our way to God's heart. Our actions and work aren't the things that make us worthy in God's eyes—it's Jesus. And it's Jesus all by himself.

Through the power of the Holy Spirit, we can no longer view our relationship with God as performance based; we instead must see it as covenant based. We will find that good works overflow from our lives from a place of security in the Father's love and in our heavenly calling.

I don't know what this moment is going to look like for you. But I want to invite you to respond to God's invitation to return. You might be reading and thinking, "I don't know if this is me," or "I'm not sure if I'm operating in my relationship with God this way." I would invite you to bring this prayer before the Lord: "Lord, if these beliefs are in me and are so hidden that I don't even realize them, please search that out of me and bring it to the surface." He invites you today to come out of hiding, stop resisting him, and come home.

Get out a pen and paper, open up a blank document, or find yourself a place on the floor to say or write these words from your heart. First, imagine his arms wide open ready to receive you. Express your need for him. Repent of your resistance. Admit all the ways you can't, and remember all the ways he can. And then? Let him love you.

Here is a prayer to help get you started:

> Lord. I do not want to stay this way. I do not want to live my life blind to all that you are. I will not live my life believing that I am enough on my own, that you do not love me, or that I can earn your love. I repent of my rebellion, and in desperation I ask you, Jesus, to forgive me and to change the way I think. I want your way. I want your love. Help me to receive it. I believe you, Jesus. I believe you will change me. Take this heart of stone that has its hands outstretched to push away, and by the power of your Holy Spirit, show me how to open them up and receive all that you are, all your love, all over me. I trust you, and I believe you. Amen.

Note

[1] Tim Keller, "The Two Prodigal Sons," accessed July 5, 2021, http://www.gracepresconway.org/uploads/1/1/9/4/119456007/discipleship_supplement_2_-_kellers_two_prodigal_sons_sermon_-_w_questions.pdf.

Chapter Two

A HEART THAT IS CENTERED

During my junior year of college, my schedule finally allowed me to pursue a lifelong dream: learning to throw pottery. I had just enough space in my schedule to take an elective of my choice, and I knew exactly what I was going to do with it. For years I had watched videos of people effortlessly making beautiful vases, bowls, and other vessels on a pottery wheel, and I was ecstatic about being able to give it a whirl.

Awestruck, I sat like a sponge as our teacher taught us the basics of making a cup on the pottery wheel. She showed us how to wedge our clay, how to constantly keep it wet, how to center it, and how to gently begin forming it into a vessel. She made it look so easy. How hard could it be? Well, if you've ever tried to make something on a pottery wheel for the first time, you can already guess how this story is probably going to go.

My clay had been carefully wedged, materials properly placed along the side of the wheel, and it was time to make something gorgeous. I slapped that ball of clay as hard as I could onto the middle of the wheel and pressed my foot on the pedal. I applied pressure in all the right places, and after a few minutes of making sure the mud lump was plastered on there, I began to pull up on the side to make the walls of the cup.

Apparently, I didn't have it secured enough because the moment I began to pull up, that ball of clay went *flying* across the studio and landed at the feet of another student two wheels away!

Oops.

Thankfully, our teacher wasn't surprised or upset one bit. As I grabbed my sopping wet ball of clay off the floor she said, "I know you want to build something, but you must center your piece before you do anything else. Learning to center correctly will probably take you a few months." Great. Well, I didn't really like the thought of producing nothing for months. So, I just kept doing my thing and quickly moved through the process only to wind up with holey pots, baseless vases, and cups that broke in the kiln because parts of the piece were too thin. Finally, my teacher informed me that my only assignment for the rest of the semester was to focus on learning to center. No building—just centering. Then the next semester, I could start building.

If you aren't familiar with pottery lingo, centering is the process of positioning your clay in the perfect middle of the wheel so it doesn't move at all. Just because it looks centered on the outside doesn't mean it's centered on the inside. It's not enough to just attach the clay to the wheel. To truly center a piece of clay, you must hover over the clay with one hand on the side of the clay and the other pressing the top as it spins around. Because the clay naturally wants to move to where there is the least resistance, the beginning of the centering process feels like trying to control a very unruly child. You must use your core muscles and arms to keep it from moving. This is a full-blown workout, y'all, let me tell you. I don't care what anybody says, you don't need a fancy workout program to get you some nice abs and biceps—just take up pottery. Once you've attached the clay to the spinning wheel, you then gently pull the clay up and down, up and down, up and down until there is absolutely no side to side or wavering movement by any part of the clay. As seen in my first pottery projects, if you skip over or hurry this process, there will be no solid foundation for the base, the walls will be uneven, and the entire piece will be wonky because there is no solid center to build from. This basic process is what I did for that entire semester.

Wedge the clay.
Give the clay no resistance.
Pull up.
Push down.
Pull up.
Push down.
Yes! Finally, no movement!
Time's up! Class is over.
Repeat.

All semester long, I practiced centering that clay, and the next semester I was able to create some truly beautiful pieces. In the middle of those very routine and mundane days of centering the clay, I felt the Lord reminding my heart that when we try to build beautiful things with our lives without centering them on the transformational power of the gospel, we will end up with an unstable foundation, uneven walls, and a vessel that is easily cracked under fire and pressure. When our lives are not centered on Jesus and the good news of the gospel, we will not be the vessels able to do what we were designed to do.

The Path of Least Resistance

Just like that unruly clay, our hearts are naturally inclined to drift toward the path that has the least resistance—that is, the path that is the most widely accepted or most familiar to us. Culturally, we are surrounded by achievement-based systems and societal norms that all lead us back to a work-to-earn mentality. This is the most natural way of thinking for many of us. We won't find resistance in carrying this mentality into our culture because this is how we earn titles, jobs, promotions, recognition, money, and even value. Taking it a step further, some of us grew up in church environments that intentionally or unintentionally encouraged behavior modification or equated good behavior with God's pleasure, and it just became another natural manifestation of this work-to-earn mentality. If society and culture work this way, it isn't hard to take our earthly patterns of thinking and marry them with how we think God works and is pleased. We won't find resistance here, because if the enemy can get us caught up in obsessing over our own works and our own merit, it will ultimately keep our eyes off Christ because they are completely centered on ourselves.

That's just it. Where our eyes begin to turn, the heart is sure to follow. What we fixate on eventually becomes the thing we drift toward—whether we mean to or not. If we aren't careful, we might accidentally drift into the waters of a distorted gospel, which is exactly what happened to the church in Galatia.

Paul, the former Christian killer turned soul winner, wrote the book of Galatians to the churches of Galatia to reiterate the truths of the gospel, which some people were trying to add to. The believers Paul wrote to had already been told the gospel, but shortly after, they began to turn away from the gospel of grace and were falling into teachings that encouraged them to follow the Law for righteousness. Let me tell you, this letter is serious business—Paul wastes no time and gets right to the point of why he is writing this important letter to them.

In the introductions of most of Paul's other letters, he spends a good bit of time telling them how thankful he is for them, how much he misses them, or refers to them as the "faithful saints" (Eph. 1:1). Yeah, the Galatian church got none of that! There were no 'atta boys or pats on the back from Paul. He spends four verses on a quick greeting and then gets right in their business, as if to say, "Whoa, whoa, whoa! What are you guys doing!" He writes:

> I am astonished that you are so quickly deserting him who called you in the grace of Christ and are turning to a different gospel—not that there is another one, but there are some who trouble you and want to distort the gospel of Christ. (Gal. 1:6–7 ESV)

Among the Galatian Christians, a group of people referred to as Judaizers had infiltrated their churches. This group of people most likely belonged to the Pharisees and were trying to convince Gentile believers that in order to be saved, the Gentiles had to be circumcised and also had to keep the Law of Moses.[1] In other words, these Judaizers were trying to add on different requirements, regulations, and rules to the gospel that was already signed, sealed, and delivered by the blood of Christ. They were taking their former way of life—adhering to the Jewish laws and customs—and trying to marry it with following Jesus. When I read this account, it can be so easy to look down on these Jewish Christians for falling for what Paul refers to as a distorted gospel after hearing the word of truth. But the truth is, we fall into the same trap when we try to marry our work-to-earn mentality with the gospel message! It's just another version of trying to "add" to what Jesus has already done. My pastor helped me recognize that this is the heart of the struggle for any long-standing Christian—to bring something in addition to Jesus. But before you know it, the gospel addition has become a gospel distortion.

These new believers were easily detached from the truth of the gospel because their lives weren't centered on it yet. Paul's letter aimed to do just that—to set them straight on their relationship to the Law, reiterate what Jesus had done for them, remind them of their standing with God, and reassure them how they could be confident in their salvation. Paul had to take these believers back to the very basics so they could build their faith on a firm foundation—one that refused any additions.

For those of us raised in church or well acquainted with the gospel story, we can find ourselves far away from the basics we once learned about. Somewhere along the way, the gospel just became a one-time confession as a seven-year-old and was no longer something we leaned on every single day. Somehow, being "saved by grace" slowly morphed into a checklist faith that no longer saw a covenantal relationship but rather a conditional one—based on all the "good" things we could do and bad things we'd promise and try not to do; all the while being convinced we were simply building big and beautiful things for God.

But the truth is, the good news of Christ goes against every natural inclination we have—even the inclination to prove our own place at his table. Even the inclinations that are seemingly "good." Jesus came to break our man-made boxes, religious categories, and labels so that we would not merely copy the patterns, behaviors, and customs of this world but that our minds would be radically transformed and renewed by the Spirit of God, so we might discern who God really is, what truly matters to him, and what his good, pleasing, and perfect will is (Rom. 12:2). The gospel introduces us to a completely new way, one that doesn't follow along with the ways our society functions. Our lives become a process of realigning and centering our hearts to the truths presented in the gospel. As we do this, we'll find that the more we surrender to his beautiful design and come into alignment with how he sees things, the more our lives become centered. Our lives consist of this constant process—remembering the gospel, aligning ourselves with the truth of God—and from that place, we build. But before we race off trying to build, let's take a step back and take some time to go back to the beginning.

Back to the Basics

Sometimes as long-time believers, we need to go back to the basics. To scrap our arsenals of religious jargon, surrender our man-made rules, investigate the pages of Scripture, and ask: Jesus—who are you? Why did you need to come? What did you do? What does that mean for the world? We need to hear the gospel all over again with fresh ears and pray that we would have eyes to truly see. Because if our hearts are not rooted, centered, and planted in the truth of the gospel, we fall prey to making our own additions and becoming disciples of a distorted one that is anything but centered on Christ.

In this book, we will take a closer look at some of the gospel distortions—or false gospels—that keep us stuck in patterns of striving, performing, and working to earn God's acceptance. These false gospels have slithered their way into the church and into the hearts of believers, while remaining totally under the radar. But before we dive into the false gospels that keep us trapped, I believe we need to go back and get reacquainted with the real gospel—the gospel that sets us free. In the next four chapters, that is exactly what we're going to do—break it down. We're going to take things all the way back to the very beginning and talk about the effects of sin, the importance of the Law, why Jesus had to come, what happens at salvation, and what happens afterward. Once we take a good hard look at what the gospel is, we will then look at what it is not.

Y'all, I am no theologian, and I'm not going to pretend to be. All I know is that the gospel is truly so simple that a small child can understand it and receive it in all its fullness. Yet, we've muddied the waters and made the gospel so complicated that it's hard to know what it is and is not.

Some of the most beautiful work happens when we start from the beginning, with a blank sheet of paper in hand, asking Jesus to do something extraordinary and brand new on it. My prayer is that we'll have eyes to see the story of God in a fresh new way since this whole thing is about him, because of him, and for him.

Before you dive into the next few chapters, will you take a moment of surrender before the Lord? Pray for your heart to be ready and open to receive all he might reveal to you. Pray that the Holy Spirit would bring clarity, guidance, and magnification of the truth. And when you're ready, let's dive in. With a blank canvas in hand and a surrendered heart, let's go back and look at the gospel that sets us free.

Note

[1] Luke writes about this same issue in the book of Acts. See Acts 15:1–5.

PART ONE

THE GOSPEL THAT SETS US FREE

We may have heard it a thousand times: the salvation ABCs or a memorized monologue of how to explain the gospel to other people. But in our Christian lives, we tend to forget. I believe this is why God commanded the Israelites to make a practice of remembering the glorious work God had done in previous generations so that they would never forget it, add to it, or take from it. As women of God, let's seek to do the same. Let's return to the Good Story and pray for eyes to see it in a fresh way. As we seek to break down the gospel into its bare bones, let's be on the lookout for ways we've added to it. Let's return to the simple gospel that is power all by itself.

Chapter Three

THE MARRING

Sometimes, when we're extremely familiar with the entire narrative of a story, it can be difficult to empathize with the characters who had no idea how the rest of the story would play out. As people who live in a time when most have a cursory understanding of the storyline of the Bible, it can be difficult to truly understand the devastation of the fall. Why? Because we know how it all works out in the end.

But they didn't.

Adam and Eve had a brief taste of intimacy, perfection, and wholeness that we have yet to experience this side of heaven. We have yet to put bare feet on the ground of a perfect Earth, unmarred and without defect.

But they did.

They tasted and saw the goodness of God in all his splendor—with clear eyes and unveiled faces. Souls living in perfect harmony with the Father, not an iota of shame, not an ounce of fear or pride. Freedom in all its fullness. I can't imagine what it's like to be in a world where nothing is separated. Where there are no walls, no defenses, no hiding, no need to cover up.

This is the kind of intimacy we long for—to both know and be known, fully loved, and fully accepted. They had it all. And we all know the plot twist—we know it well—the lie that made it all fall apart. The lie that made them question: Is God withholding something from me? Through Eve's eyes, that question marred all the beauty that was, all that had been given, and gave a great enough cause to take a bite and see if it were true: "God is not enough, but maybe I can be."

In that moment, disbelief caused the great divide. A divide humanity has tried for centuries to build a bridge over to cross. Intimacy was drastically interrupted. Arms that once embraced the Father stiffened into one hand outstretched to keep him at arm's length while the other hid their shame. Hearts once connected now went running in the opposite direction of the Father who had given them everything.

The loss they felt must have been so grave, so devastating, and so foreign. To have tasted perfection and watch it all warp in just a moment. Eyes that once looked on their bodies as free and unashamed now looked on themselves with shame and felt a desperate need to hide. This is the first example we see of someone trying to manage their own sin. One of my favorite books of all time, *The Cure*, lays out their condition plainly:

> This shame—this self-awareness of their uncleanness—prompted Adam and Eve to fashion masks from leaves to hide what they now feared was true about them.... They were both convinced something was now uniquely and terribly wrong about them, with them. This is how shame works.... Shame drives us to hide, convinced that we cannot truly be forgiven or made clean.[1]

Yet in the darkest hour, we see the first glimpse of the gospel in God's reaction. When man hid, with no desire to be found by him, God came anyway. Not hesitating in disbelief, not running in anger, not rummaging through the branches in frustration to find his wayward creation. Just walking in the cool of the day in the garden he had made (Gen. 3:8). As he walked, he called out to the man, "Where are you?" And at his call, I imagine the man and woman, heads bowed low, hands shaking to shield themselves with itchy leaves, stumbled their way out of the branches to face the One they had just betrayed.

In his kindness, he clothed them with animal skins to cover their nakedness (Gen. 3:21) but drove them out of the garden. God's two members of creation, now cursed, began their exodus into a world separated from the God of love with only a memory of the goodness they had once tasted. From here on out, the world and all who inhabited it would be marred by the effects of sin. For centuries, people would try to bridge the divide and find their way home through effort, moralism, and heroic promises. But someday, One would come who would lay down his life and cleanse humans from all that marred them—and they would walk free from the power of sin by trusting in what he paid to cleanse.

The Land before the Law

> *"Therefore, just as sin came into the world through one man, and death through sin, and so death spread to all men because all sinned."* —Romans 5:12 ESV

The onset of sin immediately revealed its contagious and contaminating nature. Scottish poet Horatius Bonar paints a beautiful word picture when he describes the infectious, universal effects of sin: "It is not like a stone dropped in a wilderness, upon the sand, there to lie motionless and powerless. It is like that same stone cast into a vast waveless lake, which raises ripple upon ripple, and sends its disturbing influence abroad, in circle after circle, for miles on every side, till the whole lake is in motion."² From here on out in the Bible narrative we see the harsh, disgusting, and disillusioning effects of sin play out. Where God designed his creation to live in harmony, we see relationships rapidly broken down by murder, deceit, sexual abuse, immorality, drunkenness, betrayal, theft, and an onslaught of other grievances. Where God designed unhindered, uninterrupted intimacy with his creation, those he made crafted gods of worldly materials, placing their hope in the inanimate. Yet in the midst of a sin-infested world, God made himself known to a few, specifically, a man named Abram (whose name God later changed to Abraham). Because of the devastating effects of sin, God would provide his people a Law to guide them in a sin-filled world. God initiated the precursor to the Law by making himself known to this man, Abram. In a world of many gods, Abram encountered the living God and was given a call and a promise:

> Now the LORD said to Abram, "Go from your country and your kindred and your father's house to the land that I will show you. And I will make of you a great nation, and I will bless you and make your name great, so that you will be a blessing. I will bless those who bless you, and him who dishonors you I will curse, and in you all the families of the earth shall be blessed." (Gen. 12:1–3 ESV)

Abraham continued to believe God, and God considered him righteous because of it (Gen. 15:6). Throughout Abraham's life and through the life of his descendants—who would become known as the Israelites—many had encounters with God and lived according to his leading. As the Israelites grew and multiplied in the land of Egypt, they became oppressed by the pharaoh at the time who was concerned about the Israelites becoming too powerful. For the next four hundred plus years, the Israelites lived under Egyptian rule, oppressed and submerged in a polytheistic, idolatrous nation. But the tides began to shift when a man named Moses came on the scene.

Moses, a Hebrew man who grew up in an Egyptian household, was called by God via a burning bush with a revelation of whom God was. God called Moses to partner with him in rescuing the Israelites from the power of the Egyptians and guiding them into a land he had set aside for his people (Exod. 3:9–10). After a long series of protests, miraculous signs, and numerous plagues, Pharaoh sent the Israelites out of Egypt. Protected by the power of God during their exodus, the Israelites spent the next forty years on a journey to this land that had been promised to them through Abraham. And on this journey, God would initiate a Law, through Moses, to govern his people for the next few centuries.

For such a long time, I found the idea of "the Law" that is referenced so many times in the New Testament incredibly confusing. Why in the world did God's people have to follow all these rules? And do we have to follow them now? These are questions that have boggled my mind as I've tried to reconcile the New Testament with the Old. For us to fully understand the history and context of the new covenant and the power of the gospel, we must understand the basis of the old covenant. This chapter holds a lot of information, but my hope is that it will help lay the foundation for our understanding of true freedom. Get comfy, grab a snack, brew some coffee, and let's dive in.

Why the Law Was Given

As we've already established, the Law was given to Moses on this journey to the promised land with the rest of Israel. Moses went up to Mount Sinai, and there, God made a covenant with the Israelites, and the Law given to Moses was the terms of this covenant. This is often referred to in the New Testament as "the Law" or

"The Mosaic Law." This Law was given specifically to the nation of Israel to guide them in righteous living, set them apart from other nations, reveal God's standard of absolute righteousness, and give direction for the nation.

If you've ever thumbed through Exodus, Leviticus, Numbers, or Deuteronomy, you are bound to have seen some commandments that make you do a double take. Let's be real—these are the books in your yearlong Bible reading plan that you lag the most in because you want to skip over them! Eyes start to cross when reading about sacrificing doves, going through multiple steps of purification, being unclean, and on and on. These laws don't make a whole lot of sense to us in our current day and age and can feel a little daunting to read, but it's important for us to understand why they are sprinkled through the Old Testament. Many theologians have suggested that the Law can be broken down into three different categories:[3]

- The Moral Law (The Ten Commandments)
- The Social/Judicial Law
- The Ceremonial Law

The Moral Law refers to the Ten Commandments, or the ethical guidelines that clearly lay out right and wrong. Jesus summarized the Moral Law with two basic commands: love God and love others (Matt. 22:37–39). The Social/Judicial Laws were the set of regulations that instructed the Israelites in how to deal with economic, political, and civil issues with one another. The Ceremonial Law gave the nation of Israel instruction for worship, directions for order in the Tabernacle, and education on what fellowship with God should look like. Essentially, the Mosaic Law would help guide the Israelites morally, in their civil interactions with one another, in economics, as well as in their ceremonial practices.

When looking at the story of the first few books of the Bible where the Law is given, you see a pattern of the Law being given to the people and their inability to keep this Law. When the Law was pronounced, rebellion was sure to follow. It was almost like putting a big red button in a room with a child and telling them, "Don't touch this!" But what do they want to do when explicitly told not to touch something? Touch it. This resulted in more laws being given and more rebellion by the people. When we read through the beginning passages of Scripture, we see that God's chosen people, no matter how many laws, rules, and regulations were given, were unable to follow the Law. With every new law that was given, the Israelites became more aware of their own sin and their own inadequacy to live up to what God required of them. This is exactly what the Law was designed to do.

To take it a step further, God's Law ultimately revealed his absolute, righteous standard—his utter holiness. This standard alone has the power to convict humanity of their sin and leave us guilty and condemned before him. But in this recognition of being totally incapable of meeting God's righteous standard, humans were left with a gaping need. A need to be rescued. A need for the gospel. The Law was given because of humanity's sin—to lead them and guide them until Christ came. It served as a mirror to point out their own sin in comparison to God's holiness. Paul clearly explains the Law's purpose in Galatians 3:19, 21–24 (NLT):

> Why, then, was the law given? It was given alongside the promise to show people their sins. But the law was designed to last only until the coming of the child who was promised. . . . If the law could give us new life, we could be made right with God by obeying it. But the Scriptures declare that we are all prisoners of sin, so we

> receive God's promise of freedom only by believing in Jesus Christ.
>
> Before the way of faith in Christ was available to us, we were placed under guard by the law. We were kept in protective custody, so to speak, until the way of faith was revealed.
>
> Let me put it another way. The law was our guardian until Christ came; it protected us until we could be made right with God through faith.

When we unpack this portion of Paul's letter, we can see that the Law had three distinct roles and purposes: to uncover sin, to confine, and act as a custodian until Christ came. Let's break these roles down.

Role #1. Uncover Our Sin (Gal. 3:19)

I'm not sure there is a better illustration for this reality than in the popular test given to young children called "The Marshmallow Experiment." Take a little breather from this content, search for the experiment on YouTube, and crack yourself up for a hot minute. In this hilarious experiment, an adult places a large marshmallow in front of a child and gives them two options: they can either eat the first marshmallow or wait patiently and when the adult comes back after fifteen minutes, they can have two. But we all know the underlying message of the instruction: don't eat the marshmallow until I come back. When the adult leaves the room, that poor child cannot help but be entirely fixated on that marshmallow. It consumes them. You'll see shots of them smelling the marshmallow, rubbing it, licking it, squeezing it, and talking about it out loud. It is incredibly entertaining! Some of the children just cannot contain themselves and eat it, while others wait it out. The comparison here is not necessarily the ability to wait for the better thing, but rather the clear evidence that is seen when a directive is given: do not eat the marshmallow. Suddenly, the child is not fixated on any other thing except that marshmallow and how bad they want to eat it. In just one moment, something was awakened with the simple word "don't." I'm convinced this is why diets never work for me because the minute I hear the word "don't" eat that, all I want to do is . . . eat that.

This is, in essence, the same reality we see in the relationship with the people of God and the Law. As Paul says in Romans 7:7–8 (ESV),

> If it had not been for the law, I would not have known sin. For I would not have known what it is to covet if the law had not said, "You shall not covet." But sin, seizing an opportunity through the commandment, produced in me all kinds of covetousness.

Clearly, our flesh has a complicated relationship with the word "don't." Therefore, the Law, which very plainly lays out what the people of God were to do and not to do, resulted in a great awakening and arousal of inward sin, with no solution in how to absolve it. The Law was merely a mirror that showed fault and blemish, but the mirror itself couldn't save.

Role #2. Confine Us (Gal. 3:23)

Not only did the Law make humankind keenly aware of their sin; it truly acted as a prison. Paul says, "We were confined under the law, imprisoned until the coming faith was revealed" (Gal. 3:23). The Law held us imprisoned to the power of our own sin that reminded us we could not follow through on what God required of us; and therefore, we stood undeniably guilty before him.

We cannot escape our own sin.

We cannot deliver ourselves from its power.

There is no amount of striving to break those prison walls because there is no way to be free from it. All who abide by the Law are cursed unless they can follow it perfectly, and we cannot (Gal. 3:10). The Law couldn't offer salvation from this predicament but only condemnation that comes from breaking what it demands.

Role #3. Act as a Custodian (Gal. 3:24)

Paul compares the Law to our "guardian" or "schoolmaster" before Christ came. Blue Letter Bible gives a description of the role of these guardians: "Among the Greeks and Romans the name was applied to trustworthy slaves who were charged with the duty of supervising the life and morals of boys belonging to the better class. The boys were not allowed so much as to step out of the house without them before arriving at the age of manhood."[4]

In other words, these temporary guardians served as moral disciplinarians over these young men, following them everywhere until they were of age and could be free of their micromanagement. In the same way, the Law served to protect and prevent Israel from sinning against God.

Feeling Hopeless Yet?

If there is anything we can take away from this, it is that if this were where the story ended, we would indeed be without hope. You may be thinking, why did God give the Law if the point of the Law was to make us hopeless? Well, in a sense it was. It was meant to make humanity not dependent on their own power, strength, will, and control. It was meant to make people aware of their imprisonment to the power of sin, enslaved to their own passion, with no human ability to deliver themselves from this predicament.

The Law was the perfect precursor for the Messiah.

The one who came to set the captives free.

Who would free people from the power of sin.

Who would give them a new heart, unmarred by the stain of sin.

Who would write the Law of God on their hearts.

Who would place in them a desire to do the will of God instead of following in their fleshly desires.

Who would remove their guilt and erase their shame.

The Law ultimately made a way for the Savior and caused in us a desperation for One who could deliver us from these prison walls and set our feet in wide open spaces—to run wild in fields of grace.

A Messiah was coming.

REFLECT & RESPOND

1. If you were to define the "old covenant" in two sentences to someone who didn't understand, how would you explain it?

2. How does the old covenant show us our need for Christ?

Notes

[1] John Lynch, Bill Thrall, and Bruce McNicol, "The Cure: What If God Isn't Who You Think He Is and Neither Are You?," in *The Cure: What If God Isn't Who You Think He Is and Neither Are You?* (Phoenix: Trueface, 2011), 20.

[2] Horatius Bonar, "The Curse," BibleHub, accessed July 8, 2021, https://biblehub.com/sermons/auth/bonar/the_curse.htm.

[3] I have found J. Hampton Keathley's discussion of this topic helpful. See "The Mosaic Law: Its Function and Purpose in the New Testament," Bible.org, June 10, 2004, https://bible.org/article/mosaic-law-its-function-and-purpose-new-testament.

[4] "Lexicon :: Strong's G3807 - *paidagōgos*," Blue Letter Bible, accessed July 8, 2021, https://www.blueletterbible.org/lexicon/g3807/kjv/tr/0-1/.

Chapter Four

THE MEDIATOR

> *"Run, John, Run! The Law commands*
> *But gives me neither feet nor hands.*
> *Far grander news the Gospel brings*
> *It bids me fly and gives me wings!"*
>
> —John Bunyan

Rumors of a coming Messiah were sprinkled through the pages of the Old Testament and burned in the minds of the Jewish people who had them committed to memory. These small glimpses and foretastes of what was to come were much like pieces of broken glass that when pieced together revealed the face and nature of Jesus, their Messiah. But many missed him because he wasn't what they expected, imagined, or anticipated. And many of us miss him today because he isn't what we expect.

Throughout the Old Testament, God called his chosen people to anticipate and be on the lookout for the coming Messiah. Right after God banished Adam and Eve from the garden, he ushered the first of many promises about the Redeemer who would come to rescue them: "And I will put enmity between you and the woman, and between your offspring and hers; he will crush your head, and you will strike his heel" (Gen. 3:15 NIV).

While sin and death would run rampant for centuries, God instituted systems and spoke directly through prophets and the Psalms; all of which testified of a future time when a rescuer would deliver a fatal blow to sin and death—once and for all. The Law of Moses, the Prophets, and the Psalms were riddled with prophesies that the Messiah would fulfill when he came. These Old Testament prophesies acted as broad strokes on a canvas made in a dimly lit room, painting a picture of the coming One who would one day flip the lights on, and everything that was a shadow would be lit up and the world would be forever changed.

The Sacrificial System

As discussed in the previous chapter, the Law was given to govern the people of Israel, to set them apart, to set a standard for God's righteousness, and to reveal both their sin and a need for someone to save them from it. Yet, embedded in the letter of the Law was a sacrificial system in which people could tangibly experience and see that there was retribution and payment needed to atone for their sins.

Through Moses, God instituted the tabernacle and eventually the temple—God's dwelling place where his presence could be found. Here, the people of Israel could worship God and encounter his presence, but also offer sacrifices as a substitution for forgiveness of their sin. This instruction was given in Leviticus 17:11 (NIV): "For the life of a creature is in the blood, and I have given it to you to make atonement for yourselves on the altar; it is the blood that makes atonement for one's life."

These sacrifices offered temporary forgiveness for specific sins but had to be repeated again and again with every wrongdoing.

These sacrifices were never meant to be the permanent solution for sin, just as the high priest was never meant to be the permanent mediator between God and humanity. There was one sacrifice in particular that happened one day every year, the Day of Atonement, when the high priest went through a series of cleansings so he could go into the Most Holy Place, the room in which God himself dwelled, separated from the rest of the rooms by a thick curtain. For this particular offering, the high priest took two goats as a sin offering for the people. One goat was sacrificed as an offering for the people's sin and the other one was let go into the wilderness to show the removal of sin (Lev. 16:15, 20–22). The entire sacrificial system painted a clear picture that forgiveness required a life for a life. This system was but a shadow of the coming One who would give his life, once and for all, for the sins of the world.

Unmet Expectations

Even while the sacrificial system was in play, God was revealing what was to come through prophets who foretold what the Messiah would be like. But here's where things got complicated: the prophecies concerning the Messiah were twofold. Although there were explicit prophesies about how Jesus would come humbly, with nothing special about his appearance, and how he would suffer and die,[1] other prophecies spoke of a conquering king who would come and set up his kingdom on earth to rule.[2] Some of those prophecies referred to Jesus's first coming, which would be as a suffering servant, and others referred to his second coming, in which he would return as conquering King.

This gives us a better backdrop as to why so many Jews—so many religious, law-following people—didn't believe the Messiah had come when Jesus finally arrived on scene. They were expecting a conquering king. At the time of Jesus's birth, the nation of

Israel had been severely oppressed for centuries by conquering kingdoms such as Babylon, Medo-Persia, Greece, and Rome.[3] Put yourself in their shoes—which Messiah would you want if you were under severe oppression from a brutal worldwide system of government? The king, right? Many Jewish people, even including some of Jesus's disciples, clung to their expectations of what he should be, what he should do, and how he could make their lives better. But from the moment he arrived, Jesus broke a thousand expectations. He broke every box people placed him in, and that's exactly what he continued to do for his entire time on earth.

To start with, the birth of the Messiah was basically an abomination—being born of an unmarried woman. An angel came to a young woman named Mary and told her she would become pregnant through divine intervention, and that she would give birth to the Son of God. Mary believed God and accepted this. When it came time for Jesus's birth, he wasn't surrounded by wealth, comfort, and luxury, but in a manger in a barn. As he grew up, his home was not among palaces and royalty, but as the son of a carpenter in a small town called Nazareth. While most couldn't tell from the looks of things, Jesus had an otherworldly nature—the fullness of God in his Spirit, while embodying all the parts of being a human.

When his ministry began, he drew no attention to the wonders he performed. Instead of surrounding himself with the religious elite, he chose to spend his time around prostitutes, sinners, and tax collectors, not those of piety. As he made claims about who he was and what he came to do, those who should have recognized him as the Messiah—the Jews and religious leaders who knew the Scriptures—refused to believe him because he wasn't what they expected. The Jews were expecting a king by their definition—one who would conquer their very real oppressors, stand up for justice, and reign—not die.

Oddly enough, of all the people who "missed" Jesus, it was the Pharisees who were the most blind-sighted and resistant to him. In Jesus's day, the Pharisees were the religious elite, those who professed to be the most passionate about the truth of God. You could say the Pharisees were extreme rule followers and Law abiders who took God's Law very seriously. In fact, they took it so seriously that they essentially put guard-rails around the Law to prevent themselves from breaking any of the Law's commands. They created supplementary purity rules and laws to give off the appearance of godliness and projected these onto other people. The Pharisees, in a sense, distorted the truth about God by elevating and clinging to their man-made religion. When it came to following rules, these people were extra—and not in a good way. They took more delight in their pious, holier-than-thou posture than in God himself. As a result, when God in the flesh stood right in front of their eyes, they missed him because they didn't know him. These religious role models expected Jesus to be passionate about adherence to the Law, in agreement with their "extra" pursuit of righteousness, and segregated from sinners like they were. But instead, Jesus made claims about coming to fulfill the Law, he scorned the religious for their man-made systems and religiosity, and he welcomed and hung around the sinners.

To take it a step further, Jesus didn't single out well-versed, pious prodigies to be his apprentices. No, he chose unqualified and uneducated men to be his disciples, his apprentices with whom he spent most of his time. These men left everything to follow him. And day by day, he continued to show them who he was, and what he came to do. He made it very clear during his earthly ministry that he had one mission and Hebrews 10:5–7 (NIV) lays it out clearly:

> Sacrifice and offering you did not desire, but a body you prepared for me; with burnt offerings and sin offerings you were not pleased. Then I said, "Here I am—it is written about me in the scroll—I have come to do your will, my God."

Jesus came to live on earth so he could die. For Jesus had come to do away with what had been and to bring about something brand new: a new covenant between God and man. End goal. Even the disciples had unmet expectations: a Messiah with so much heavenly power shouldn't die. But that is exactly what he came to do.

People crafted so many molds for how Jesus should be, how he should act, and what he should deem important; but this Jesus—he was a mold breaker, refusing to submit to anyone's earthly expectations of him. And my friends, he is still breaking molds today—the molds we make. As Christians, we tend to project molds of what we think Jesus should be—molds that think and look a whole lot like us, and not much like him. When we take a good, hard look at who Jesus is, we see that he is kind of wild. I love that about him. He was and is divergent in every way: bold but gentle; kind but courageous; slow to anger but firm in his justice; all loving and all truthful. He broke so many expectations in the best, most glorious way. May we make it our prayer that he would daily break our molds and expectations that we may see him rightly and emulate him clearly.

The Death to End All Death

The prophets of old talked about a time when the Messiah would bring about something entirely new. He came to bring about a new covenant—to not just do away with a system that required sacrifice to be made right with God temporarily, but to become the sacrifice, satisfying the wrath of God, so that humanity and

God could be restored permanently. But the gateway to this new life meant death to the old one—a fulfillment of the old covenant. Jesus came to be the doorway into this new life, but it would require his life—and he came to lay it down. And although Jesus was frequently blamed by those around him, namely the religious leaders, he stood blameless before God. In Jesus's thirty-three years of life on earth, he lived without sin or fault. No one had ever been able to do this. But he did.

His claims about being the Son of God, his teachings on a kingdom coming, and the way he interacted with the world around him infuriated the political and religious leaders of his day. Though they frequently tried to trap him in his words or find an excuse to kill him, they couldn't. That was, until the time was set for Jesus to do what he came to do.

One of his very own disciples betrayed him for thirty pieces of silver, and with a kiss, Jesus was delivered into the hands of some of the most ruthless men at the time. While most expected a king to fight back and demand justice, Jesus did not. When he was arrested and put on trial, he didn't defend himself. Because he didn't come for his life to be taken, but for his life to be given.

As soon as Jesus was arrested, his disciples scattered, some even denied they knew him. Jesus went to the cross completely alone yet surrounded by those who wanted him dead. Arrested and sent to his death on the grounds of blasphemy, Jesus was first beaten, bruised, battered, and mocked mercilessly. He was unrecognizable. Tattered and torn from head to toe, Jesus then had to carry his own cross up Calvary hill, bearing the weight of the cross upon which he would be hung to die. Even while men yelled horrible things at him, he prayed under his breath that God would not smite them but forgive them. Strung between two criminals, Jesus died a long, brutal death.

We Put Him There

As people reading this story centuries later, it is so easy to shake our heads at these religious leaders and people who betrayed him, sent him to trial, and were responsible for his death. But we know the narrative. We know that Jesus's life wasn't taken—it was given. All these things happened so that Jesus might fulfill what was written about him in the Law and foretold by the prophets. Jesus's crucifixion and death were a tangible, fleshed out representation of our sin. As it was written in Isaiah 53:4–5 (NIV):

> Surely he took up our pain and bore our suffering, yet we considered him punished by God, stricken by him, and afflicted. But he was pierced for our transgressions, he was crushed for our iniquities; the punishment that brought us peace was on him, and by his wounds we are healed.

Through his death, Jesus became the sacrifice that took on the full weight, penalty, shame, and destructiveness of the sins of the world. In Jesus's utter destruction we see what our sin caused. Jesus, the spotless, sinless Lamb, laid down his life so that he could embody the sin we all deserved to destroy us, take on the wrath of God that we were supposed to experience, suffer the separation from the Father that it caused, and endure the death we deserved to die. We are the people who put him there. Our sin. Our shortcomings. Our self-righteousness. Us. You. Me. And there on the cross, he made the great exchange we still can't stop talking about.

The Great Exchange

Earlier on the day Jesus died, darkness covered the land. At three in the afternoon, in a loud voice, Jesus cried out, "My God, my God, why have you forsaken me?" (Matt. 27:46 ESV). Shortly after, he was given a drink of sour wine, and then he cried out one final time: "It is finished" (John 19:30). He gave up his Spirit and took his final breath. At that moment, the ground began to shake, and miles away the walls of the Temple shook and the curtain that separated the Holy Place from the rest of the building was torn in two, right down the middle, from top to bottom (Matt. 27:51). The dividing wall between God and man was broken down through Jesus's body. The sin that separated God and humans was now bridged by the Messiah, the great mediator between God and his people. The work Jesus came to do, the old covenant he said he had come to fulfill, was finished, completed, done.

Three days later, two women went to Jesus's tomb. While they were there, a giant earthquake shook the land, and an angel came down and rolled the stone back from the entrance of the tomb. The guards who were watching fainted as the angel reported to the two women, "He is not here! He has risen!" As the women were on their way to tell the disciples, Jesus himself appeared to them, and they couldn't believe their eyes. There he was, in all his splendor and glory, risen from the grave. Jesus's resurrection sealed the deal on this great exchange: Jesus forgave all our sins—took on the charges of sin against us so we wouldn't stand condemned by them.

This is the Good News. The bad news is that our sinful nature was a lethal offense to a holy God. We were, by nature, children of wrath who deserved the wrath of God. But God in his kindness made a way for us to be reconciled to him by giving his only Son, the Son he loved, as a sacrifice to put sin to death once and for all. No longer would sacrifice be needed to repeatedly atone for our sins—this was a fulfillment of the old covenant and the dawn of a new one.

Where sin marred our story, our flesh, and our relationships with the Father and each other, Jesus stepped in as our divine mediator. Jesus—a man of sorrows and a man of many broken expectations, came to do what was far beyond what we could ever anticipate or hope, and he did it once and for all.

Believing in the Bridge

Jesus's death and resurrection sealed the new covenant: that those who receive and believe in Jesus's sacrifice are no longer under the Law, but under grace instead. Jesus offers us the gift of salvation, to be saved by him and be forever with him. We receive this gift through belief in Jesus by trusting in the sufficiency of what he's done—that the payment for our sin has been satisfied—and then we receive new life that is available in him. Through the power of the Holy Spirit, which is given to all believers, we are equipped with power to follow God as his children, we're given a new heart, and we receive an inheritance in heaven—where we will spend the rest of our eternity with God.

Jesus, the one and only true mediator, came to be the bridge. The bridge that came to reconcile a wayward world to the heart of the Father. A bridge that called the rebellious and the religious, the doubter and the do-gooder, the sinner and the self-righteous to leave their lives of self-sufficiency and self-absorbency and every good or bad thing they have done, and cross over into the Way—the way of the Father.

We can't take anything with us on that bridge. Not the good, that we may say we earned our way to the Father, and not the bad, that we may remain convinced the Father cannot love us. He asks that we drop it all and carry a cross instead, following in his wake. The way of Jesus is less and less about us conveniently fitting Jesus into our man-made boxes, and more of us bowing low in humility, denying ourselves, and beholding truth to become like him. Jesus is the most precious gift. As if the removal of our sin that stood before him wasn't enough, he took it a step further and did something even more gracious on our behalf.

REFLECT & RESPOND

1. Jesus is the bridge to the Father. On this bridge, we can't carry the good or the bad we've done; we must carry a cross instead. Do you find yourself trusting in the good things you've done to make yourself right with God? Or do you find yourself caught up in your past or the wrong things you've done, keeping you from the Father?

2. Have you found yourself trying to create molds of Jesus that look more like you and less like him? What has this looked like in your life?

Notes

[1] Read through Isaiah 53 to see prophecies about the Suffering Servant.

[2] See verses such as Zechariah 14:4, 2 Samuel 7:12–13, Daniel 7:13–14, Isaiah 9:7, Psalm 110:4, Zechariah 9:9, and Psalm 2:7.

[3] Michael Wise, "Suffering Servant or Conquering King?," Salvation Wise, accessed July 8, 2021, https://www.salvationwise.org/suffering-servant-or-conquering-king/.

Chapter Five

THE MENDING

I used to have this vivid picture in my head of what walking with God looked like. God and I stood on opposite sides of one another, with a large gap in the middle of us, engaged in a weird type of spiritual salsa dance. When I sought God in the Scriptures every day, prayed regularly, shared my faith, attended church, and maybe even some extra—I envisioned him taking steps toward me. Doing these things made me feel righteous and free to come close. But when I sinned, failed, or slipped up, it felt like I took two steps backward, and so did he. Each day felt like a back-and-forth salsa, trying to close the space between myself and the Father. I remember praying so often, "Lord, please help me close this space between you and I, so that I can be as close as possible to you." I was determined to close the gap, and I thought the way to do that was by "working on my sin" and choosing better next time. In my head, this formula could ensure the closeness I was looking for: right living + wrong avoiding = right standing.

In some seasons, I was completely convinced that my hard-earned intentionality unlocked doors to come before the throne of God. I had something tangible to prove why I was worthy to be close to him. Yet in others, when my intentionality, discipline, and an unstained reputation weren't there, I was equally convinced of God's disappointment in me and distance from me. I had nothing to bring before the throne of God. As a result, I thought he backed away from me because I backed up from him.

If you've ever lived in a season of this kind of spiritual salsa dance, you know that it is entirely formulaic, predictable, measurable—which is great: you're always aware of your perceived standing with God. Yet, your soul knows all too well that this type of tango is incredibly disheartening. You never feel for long that the space is erased, because you're always causing it with your inconsistency.

I have reason to believe so many of us aren't living freely in the life God has planned for us because we are in bondage to the belief that we are the ones responsible for closing the chasm between ourselves and the Father, even though we swear, profess, and confess that Jesus came to do that. Yet here we are, stuck on a hamster wheel of trying to prove our allegiance, convinced that somehow our well-intentioned devotion might close the great divide.

What if I told you that this spiritual salsa of striving, proving, earning right standing with God is antigospel? As we talked about in the last chapter, Jesus is our mediator—our substitute—taking the penalty of our sin that we fully deserve by paying for it with his life. But the good news doesn't end there—it keeps getting better. In his death and resurrection, a life changing transaction took place. The right standing between people and the Father that was broken in the garden was restored fully through the person of Jesus Christ on the cross. Jesus's death made a way for us to be, as the New Testament introduces, justified. This act of justification calls for a screeching halt to our patterns of striving that seek to somehow earn right standing with the Father through works of our own hands. It is a gift, not to be repaid through good intentions and right living, but to be received humbly by our empty hand.

A Radical, Unbelievable Gift

Striving, proving, and climbing ladders can easily become part of our relationship with God because we often use these strategies in our everyday lives. It is the currency of our culture. Our prior performances, reputations, and resumes have the potential to unlock and open doors for us to get connected with whomever we desire. If I am looking to move up in my career and look for a bigger job, I will pull out my resume, full of my prior experiences, prestigious recognitions, and a list of reasons why I am worthy to be accepted for the job. If I'm trying to further my education and get into a good college, I submit a transcript that reflects my grades and performance in academic classes, essays that describe my qualifications, and a list of involvements that prove my dedication to my community. In both scenarios, if the person on the other side of the desk finds me good enough, qualified, and worthy, I will be accepted based on what I have put forward.

Understandably, many of us carry this mentality into how we view God. Both historically and in the present, so many, including myself, have believed that if we want a true connection with the Father, we must yank out our ethical, moral, and behavioral resumes to try to prove that we are worthy and enough to have a close connection with him.

But in Romans 3:21–22, Paul announces a countercultural reality that puts every ethical resume and moral record we could offer to shame. He affirms that there is a righteousness that has been revealed apart from the Law that comes through faith in Jesus to all who believe. A type of righteousness that is received, not earned. A righteousness that comes not from adhering to the Law, but upon belief in the Son of God. Paul goes on to say, "For all have sinned and fall short of the glory of God; they are justified freely by his grace through the redemption that is in Christ Jesus" (vv. 23–24).

This justification, my friends, crushes, obliterates, and renders useless our need to strive.

Not only are we forgiven; we are justified freely.

What does this mean?

According to Blue Letter Bible, the word "justify" means "to declare, pronounce, one to be just, righteous, or such as he ought to be."[1]

Being justified is so much more than just being forgiven. In fact, if we reduce our salvation to merely being forgiven, we are missing the gospel because it is so much more than that! Think of it this way: if this were in a court of law, forgiveness is the cancelling of a debt. It's the removal of the punishment that our actions 100 percent deserved and earned. Justification takes it a step further. It is a declaration. It's a pronouncement, made by God, that not only are we forgiven, we are legally deemed righteous in his sight, as we ought to be, because of Jesus.

Because in this great exchange, all that we did, all that we earned, the judgement that we accrued, was placed on Jesus on the cross. In exchange, all that he did, the victories he won, the righteousness he lived out, his right standing before the Father, was given to us, pronounced over us. It's not just a removal of sins, it is a bestowal of the righteousness of Christ upon us. In the same way that Jesus became actual sin, we become actual righteousness. To be clear, this is not a process of being made righteous on the inside; this is an instantaneous declaration of righteousness over us because of the work of Jesus. Being justified means we cannot be tried over and over for our sins—we are in a permanent state of righteousness before the Father.

Many theologians refer to this righteousness as imputed. Dictionary.com defines "impute" as meaning "to attribute (righteousness, guilt, etc.) to a person or persons vicariously."[2] By having the righteousness of Christ attributed to us, we are now seen as sinless, as Jesus is sinless. You might object, "But I don't feel righteous most of the time!" This is because we are not righteous in and of ourselves; rather, all of Christ's righteousness is given to us, and this is what God sees when he brings us into relationship. Where our sin rendered us guilty, Jesus now declares us righteous.

Pretty Little Justifiers

If the gospel says we are truly justified—declared righteous— because of Christ and what he has done, that means we must resolve that there are absolutely no grounds on which we can justify ourselves before God.

None.

When we understand the reality that we are justified because of Jesus, we stop trying to "good deed" our way into God's good graces. We understand that Jesus is the gate by which we get to the Father—the bridge by which we enter freely (John 10:9).

Yet so many times, we think we understand the reality of forgiveness but then fall into this thinking: *Well, now that I'm forgiven, I really need to get my act together and live a good life for Jesus.* It's this same type of thinking Paul called the Galatians out for when he questioned them: "After beginning by the Spirit, are you now finishing by the flesh?" (Gal. 3:3).

In one of my favorite sermons, "Justified by Faith," Tim Keller paints a picture of the harmful cycle this thinking causes. He starts out by describing the person who comes to church and understands they are forgiven, but then enters this cycle of trying to live a good life like they think they should. They try and try to live a moral life, then they fall away or fail in some way. Then they recommit their lives to God and ask for forgiveness. They start the spiritual salsa dance cycle all over again by trying to live a good life, failing, asking for forgiveness, and recommitting. If you'll notice, the entire focus of this kind of cycle is on one's own sin. There is no security in this cycle because it is completely dependent on you and making sure you're earning or maintaining your forgiveness.

Ironically, he goes on to challenge the listeners stuck in a similar type of pattern to shift their focus away from sin and instead onto their boasting. Keller says:

> But I want you to consider this: that Pharisees are very concerned about their sins. Pharisees are self-justifying, moral, legalistic, miserable people. Pharisees, when they sin, they are very upset. They repent, they confess their sins, and when they're all done, they're still Pharisees. They're not Christians. Here's what will make you a Christian: don't look at your sins; look at your boasting. Look at what you boast in. Look at the things that are your justification. Look at the things that you look at and say, "That justifies my existence"; "That validates me"; "That's what makes me worthy." Paul says, "Where is boasting?" Free justification destroys it.... What makes you a Christian is not so much you repent of your sins; you should repent of your sins, but that could just make you just another Pharisee. What makes you a Christian is that you repent of your justification. Your false justification. Your false righteousness.[3]

Yikes. It is second nature for some of us to validate ourselves based on what we do. When our sin doesn't look that bad, it's because we're weighing it against what we've done right. We are justifying ourselves before God. But I love how Paul puts an end to this argument by saying: "Can we boast, then, that we have done anything to be accepted by God? No, because our acquittal is not based on obeying the law. It is based on faith. So we are made right with God through faith and not by obeying the law" (Rom. 3:27–28 NLT).

There are no grounds to boast about. This calls for us to not only repent of our sin, but to repent of the things we've believed in our hearts have justified us—our pretty little justifiers. These are things we meditate on in our hearts that cause us to breathe out a sigh of relief, convincing us that these actions are our saving graces. These could be as small as our good intentions, experienced biblical background, kind demeanor toward others, wisdom, involvement in ministry, quiet times with the Lord, or our dedicated discipline. We can even go so far as to find justification based on our healthiness—our eating habits, exercise consistency, and maintenance of our bodies. All these things aren't bad things; they are good things! But they cannot and will not justify us—ever.

When we build our lives on a foundation of pretty little justifiers for our righteousness, we will feel the internal drive to strive. Because we will always have to be laying something down. It's like being on a treadmill that asks and asks and asks of you to prove, and it will never stop. But the righteousness of Christ is a rock that cannot be moved. Why? Because Jesus said, "It is finished," and then sat down at the right hand of God. The work he did to make us right before God is done. And we can rest in that. Just as the hymn of old says: "On Christ the solid rock I stand, all other ground is sinking sand."[4]

Catalytic Results

In earlier chapters, we talked about how the Law acted like a prison that shut us up with no hope. I like to think of the Law as a hamster wheel. If we live by the Law, the deal is that in order to be made right under the Law, you cannot break it. You cannot even break it in your heart! You must keep running on this wheel until you can escape it through perfection. Which we all know would be—never. We would be running forever. But because Jesus was able to do this, he frees us from the power of the Law. He takes us off this hamster wheel so we can stop striving to be righteous and start living in his righteousness. Instead of running to be made right with God, we're running because we've been made right with him.

One morning as I was reading my Bible, I came across this verse in Hosea that finally put this revelation into language I could understand. It says: "Let's strive to know the LORD. His appearance is as sure as the dawn. He will come to us like the rain, like the spring showers that water the land" (Hosea 6:3). This verse was a reminder to redirect my striving. To realize that as long as I'm running, striving, proving, and pleasing my way to God, I will forever feel caught on a hamster wheel and chasing this idea of being "enough." However, when we understand that we are justified freely because of Christ, we understand that we have no grounds to stand on when it comes to our own righteousness. We've given up. We're done running—done trying to make our own righteousness count. We can rest in the truth that we are not enough. This is not a self-deprecating thing; it's a freedom thing. We are declared righteous in the sight of God because of Jesus, and therefore, we are freed from striving because we receive his enough-ness.

When we compare our relationship with God to a spiritual salsa dance consisting of mutual steps forward and back, we are viewing God through the lens of our own shame. Our presumed failure will always stand right in between us. But when we take hold of the Good News that our sin has been removed as far as the east from the west (Ps. 103:12) and trust that despite our best efforts and worst failures, we are declared righteous in the sight of God, our lives truly change. We begin to believe that "every moment of every day, fused with you, there He is. He never moves, never covers His ears when you sin, never puts up a newspaper, never turns His back. He's not over on the other side of your sin, waiting for you to get it together so you can finally be close. That's why they call it Good News!"[5]

With a foundation of our faith placed on the finished work of Jesus, we are free to live for God. Out of hearts changed by the Holy Spirit, good works flow from our lives as we live as ambassadors declaring a radical grace and a resurrection. We aren't bound by chains of being "good enough"; our assurance is that Christ is enough. Therefore, we can freely run, leaning into the Holy Spirit to lead us into the good works that were planned for us to walk in (Eph. 2:10). Instead, we can redirect this striving into knowing him by seeking his face and knowing his heart. In all this, please hear me say that spiritual disciplines are absolutely important and necessary. I am not saying to neglect these things or throw them out, by any means. Where striving can morph spiritual disciplines into obligations for righteousness, Jesus models how these spiritual disciplines are privileged, divine opportunities to align our hearts and minds with the will of God that we may mature in our understanding of him. When we are certain of our position in Christ, things like Bible reading, prayer, serving, meeting together in churches, and other spiritual practices are not about earning right standing with God but about enjoying him, having intimacy with him, being formed into his image and example, and loving him! The cry of spiritual disciplines is, "May Christ be formed in me!" Spiritual disciplines are not a have to, they are a get to! And as we pursue these spiritual disciplines, we can rest assured that his presence and his pleasure with us are not moving targets. It says his appearance is sure as the dawn—it is always there.

Friends, may we allow the Lord to redirect our striving today. May we ask the Holy Spirit to lead us into a rich understanding that Jesus *is* our righteousness. We don't have to run for it; we can walk in it. When we do, everything about our lives changes. Our good works and spiritual disciplines no longer come from a place of trying to "prove" our righteousness; rather, they become the proof of it. Our works will reflect that we are operating out of a changed heart that has been washed, cleansed, and regenerated by Christ. We no longer walk in the strength of our flesh, but in the reality of our new nature. This foundation unquestionably changes everything and sets the framework for Christ to start regenerating us from the inside to become more like him.

REFLECT & RESPOND

1. What are some of the "pretty little justifiers" in your own life? What kind of "resumes" do you find yourself pulling out before the Father to convince yourself (and God) of your own righteousness?

2. What would it look like for you to redirect your striving into knowing God instead of trying to prove yourself to him?

Notes

[1] "Lexicon :: Strong's G1344 - *dikaioō*," Blue Letter Bible, accessed July 9, 2021, https://www.blueletterbible.org/lexicon/g1344/kjv/tr/0-1/.

[2] Dictionary.com, s.v. "impute," https://www.dictionary.com/browse/impute.

[3] Tim Keller, "Justified by Faith," Gospel in Life, March 8, 2009, https://gospelinlife.com/downloads/justified-by-faith-5994/.

[4] Mote Edward, "My Hope Is Built on Nothing Less," Hymnary, accessed July 9, 2021, https://hymnary.org/text/my_hope_is_built_on_nothing_less#Author.

[5] Lynch, Thrall, and McNicol, *The Cure*, 33.

Chapter Six

THE MATURING

With coffee in one hand and keys in the other, my tired hand flicked the light on as my eyes darted to the left corner of my classroom. What was supposed to be a beautiful, joyful outcome to a butterfly-growing experiment ended up looking more like a bloody crime scene. Yes, there were colorful butterflies flying all around our butterfly garden, but there was red blood splattered everywhere. (At least, I thought it was blood at the time.) This shocking aftermath raised dozens of questions from my little second graders (not to mention myself) as they came in the door:

"Is that butterfly poop?"

"Did the cocoons cut the butterflies on the way out?"

"Did one of them get eaten and that is their blood?!"

"Mrs. Garrison—are those butterfly GUTS?!"

The truth was: I had no idea what was happening. Honestly, I didn't know anything about butterflies at all. I was a first-year teacher pretending like I knew what I was talking about most of the time (sorry, parents—I know better now). The extent of my butterfly knowledge was basically the summation of *The Hungry*

Little Caterpillar. All throughout this unit, I responded to sincere questions from my students with ludicrous answers:

> **Student:** "What is the caterpillar doing while it's in the cocoon?"
> **Me:** "Sleeping until it's ready to come out!"
> **Student:** "How does the caterpillar become a butterfly?"
> **Me:** "It just sheds its top layer of skin and underneath are the butterfly parts!"
> **Student:** "Why is the cocoon wiggling?!"
> **Me:** "The caterpillar is pushing against the cocoon so its wings will come out!"

But alas, the whole butterfly "blood" thing had my students (and me) very curious about this entire butterfly process. This bloody question led my students and me down a rabbit hole, completely engrossed in science videos, documentaries, and tons of pictures of the process of metamorphosis. Well, we learned all right. Not only did we learn, but we were also scarred for life. In those learning moments, all I wanted to do was write to dear Eric Carle and ask him to seriously consider changing the title of *The Hungry Little Caterpillar* to *The Texas Chainsaw Massacre*. (Also, for those still wondering about what the "bloody" stuff was, it was just the remains of the caterpillar that weren't needed to make the butterfly. Basically, unwanted leftovers. Gross.)

But good gosh, I had no idea what was happening in those little wrinkled sacs in the corner of my classroom. My fascination with the metamorphosis process in the cocoon led me into hours of studying caterpillars during one of my summer breaks. With my eyes glued to the computer, I found myself gasping, hooping, hollering, and borderline crying at what I was discovering. I could not believe the transformative secret hidden in these little creatures. God, in his kindness, used what was elementary to most to communicate life-changing truths that taught me how to rest in Christ as he transforms the innermost parts of my life.

I'm Saved—Now What?

There's a common saying, "God helps those who help themselves," and many times this is the essence of what we believe about our lives after we become Christians. I held the personal belief that because Jesus went out of his way to die for me, I should spend my life adhering to a new set of rules to pay him back for what he did. It was almost as if Christ had given me a reason to work hard, and so I should spend the rest of my life modifying my behavior and putting my nose to the grinder trying to outwardly look like him, be like him, and act like him.

But this is not at all what the gospel teaches us. The gospel proclaims undeserved freedom, not a pay-it-forward type of religion. While this "pay-it-forward" mentality might sound good in theory, this type of theology ends up stunting our maturity instead of fueling it. "If all we bring to God is our moral striving, we're back at the same lie that put us in need of salvation. We're stuck with our independent talents, longing, and resolve to make it happen. This self-sufficient effort to assuage a distant deity—it nauseates God."[1]

God has invited us not to a life of self-willed, outward behavior modification, but to a Spirit-led process of maturing into the new creation he has already made us to be. As discussed in the last chapter, part of our salvation experience is being justified in Christ, declared righteous before God. This is not a process—it's a position. Therefore, our status before the Father is righteous, and we are at peace with him—our salvation is secure (Rom. 5:1). But another part of our salvation experience is being given a completely new nature. This is not something we can fabricate through discipline, but rather something that is put in motion solely by our Creator. It is written, "If anyone is in Christ, he is a new creation. The old has passed away; behold, the new has come" (2 Cor. 5:17 ESV). Our old nature—one that was a slave to sin, motivated to live for self, and at enmity with God—has been put to death and buried with Christ (Gal. 2:20). But our new life in Christ doesn't consist of following new rules, it consists of getting a new heart. Our new heart is indwelled with the Spirit of Christ (Rom. 8:9), who gives us new motivations, convicts us, rebukes us, comforts us, and empowers us to live for Christ. The Spirit doesn't just give us the how to, he gives us the desire to! With the Spirit of God now inhabiting our hearts, we enter into a lifelong process of "being transformed into his image" (2 Cor. 3:18 NIV) and putting on "the new self, which is being renewed in knowledge after the image of its creator" (Col. 3:10 ESV).

Insert the tricky language: "being renewed." The Greek word for "renewed" in this passage (*anakainoō*) means to make new again or to become mature. Because the verb is in present passive tense, this means the process of being renewed is continual, but the action of renewal is being done *to* the subject but not *by* the subject. In other words, we are being renewed by God, and not by our own doing. Most people refer to this process as sanctification, which, unlike justification, is an ongoing process rather than a declared position. Sanctification is the continual process of spiritual rebirth God enacts in our hearts as we walk with him.

However, justification and sanctification present a salvific reality that is difficult to comprehend, in my opinion. Being justified and sanctified means I am declared righteous before God but also am being made holy at the same time. It's like—which one am I?! It's a delicate balance of the already and the not yet, which doesn't make a whole lot of earthly sense. Luckily, this complex reality of sanctification and the "already and not yet" is beautifully hidden in God's brilliant design of the butterfly.

For since the creation of the world God's invisible qualities—his eternal power and divine nature—have been clearly seen, being understood from what has been made. (Rom. 1:20 NIV)

Maturing through Metamorphosis

Funnily enough, in Romans 12:2 when Paul talks about being transformed by the renewing of your mind, the Greek word here for "transform" is *metamorphoō*. Coincidence? I think not! The process of a caterpillar morphing into a butterfly is not as cut and dry as I had originally thought. The more I dig into it, the more I want to just lay flat on the floor in awe of God. Let's get into it!

At the very beginning of a caterpillar's life, when it is still developing in its egg, it is born with something called imaginal discs, which are basically cells, or blueprints, that hold the information of the butterfly. These discs are essentially the building blocks for the new adult body parts it will need as a mature butterfly. There are imaginal discs for its eyes, its wings, its legs, and more.[2] However, these discs remain completely dormant until the caterpillar is ready to go through metamorphosis in the chrysalis. These discs are physically present in the caterpillar's body, but they are not activated. Once the caterpillar has wrapped itself in its cocoon and is ready for metamorphosis, the craziness begins. The caterpillar begins releasing digestive enzymes, leading to the disintegration and dissolving of its whole body (minus the stomach and breathing tube). So essentially, if I had cut a cocoon midmelt (as some of my students wanted me to), we would have experienced an eruption of dead-but-alive caterpillar soup. However, during this meltdown (no pun intended), the imaginal discs within the caterpillar's body do not disintegrate; rather, they are activated and begin to multiply. According to an article on Scientific American, these discs actually "use the protein-rich soup all around them to fuel the rapid cell division required to form the wings, antennae, legs, eyes, genitals and all the other features of an adult butterfly."[3]

In one tiny chrysalis, we see both death and life existing at the exact same time. As part of the caterpillar is dying away, another part is coming to life—coming into what it was designed to be. Not only this, but the death of one part of its body is actually fueling life in another. The new creature isn't an improved model of the old or a fixed-up modification of the former body—it is something entirely different. Furthermore, the new, mature body parts will also change the creature from having caterpillar behaviors to butterfly behaviors. It will no longer look on the ground and on sticks for its food; it will fly for it. Instead of having a huge appetite for leaves, it will have a smaller appetite for nectar. While opportunities for discovery used to be small due to being able to see only in black and white, it will now see in full color with compound vision.[4]

The transformation is truly one from the inside out. This little creature is dying to what it used to be while becoming what it is supposed to be—all in one little cocoon! This metamorphic process is highly comparable to what it looks like to mature in our Christian walk. When we begin our life in Christ, we are declared righteous. It's like being born again with new DNA—having imaginal cells of a righteous person, the righteousness of Jesus. The righteous DNA is present and ultimately defines what we are, but we are in the process of maturing into those righteous behaviors and characteristics. In the meantime, our old self is dying and dissolving daily. Our patterns of thinking fade, our appetites dim, our old ways of living become less alluring, and we are no longer controlled by our flesh and its demands. And at the same time, the Holy Spirit is generating new desire, a new way of thinking, and empowerment to carry out the things that honor Christ and bring him glory. We are experiencing death to self and life in Christ in the same, earthly body. We don't mature completely overnight—it is a long process of dying to self, maturing into the characteristics of our new nature, and being active participants to what God is doing in us. As Christ transforms our inner life, our values, behaviors, and actions are sure to follow. Furthermore, just as the caterpillar doesn't lose its memory of what it used to be, we don't somehow forget our past mistakes, failures, and shortcomings when we receive a new nature. However, our past mistakes can fuel our future ministry because they demonstrate the undeniable, radical grace of God to a world that is desperate for redemption.

So . . . What about Sin?

Does this mean that once we have a new nature we will not sin or struggle with sin? Of course not! We are still very much aware of and in contact with our old self, but we are not controlled by it anymore. Just as the caterpillar is not under the authority of its dissolving old body, appetites, or bodily functions, we are not ruled by our flesh because it is dead. We have been given a new identity: one that isn't defined by sin but is declared righteous. One that isn't in bondage to sin but is obedient to Christ. Instead, we can submit to and come into agreement with the Holy Spirit's leading and refining. He is eager to actively regenerate new life inside of us when we commit to the process of being renewed. This isn't a totally passive process; we still have a choice to think and act within the confines of our old sin nature or align with our new one, which the Spirit in us helps us do. As we abide, we slowly transform and display attributes of Christ as we learn to walk in these identities. Yet, as we grow and mature, we will still demonstrate immature behaviors and can still choose sin. There will be many times when we start trying to grovel on the floor for food instead of using our wings to fly for it. We will, at times, engorge ourselves on leaves that fueled our old self instead of feasting on what is light and nutritious to our new self.

But when it comes to sin, when we are stuck in patterns of striving, we are ultimately stuck in hiding. We see sin as something we need to manage, hide, resist, and control ourselves. But in trying to control it, we tend to become hyperfixated on it, awakening it rather than putting it to death. This entire cycle of "managing our sin" happens in the dark, where nobody sees. But if we have been delivered from the power of sin through the Spirit, how are we supposed to continue to fight sin without the Spirit? We can't! As believers, we are called to walk in the light—called to live with our hearts under a bright spotlight rather than in a dark shadow (1 John 1:7). When we live in the light, we are free to tattle on ourselves, both to God and our community, and no longer defend our flesh.

Our old self is dead and dissolving—but still enticing. We understand that our flesh can still tempt us, but it cannot overpower us beyond what we can endure (James 1:14; 1 Cor. 10:13). But when we do sin, we are free to confess our sin to other people and to our Father, who is faithful to forgive us and cleanse us from all unrighteousness (1 John 1:9). But as believers, as those who are being transformed by Christ, we do not make a practice of sinning (1 John 3:4–10). But the beauty of our new life in the light is that, yes, we can confess our sin to God and one another, but we can even bring our unhealthy thoughts, beliefs, and temptations before God and each other before we even carry out the sin. This process of confessing even our thoughts breaks the power of sin because it takes it straight to the light where it cannot linger.

Walking in Our New Identity

You might be thinking: *So does God do all the work, and I just sit back and let him do it?* Not exactly. I love how Nathan Bingham of Ligonier Ministries explains this: "God's method of sanctification is neither activism (self-reliant activity) nor apathy (God-reliant passivity), but human effort dependent on God."[5] With grace-driven effort, we pursue holiness and godliness with an understanding that God began and authored this work in us, and he will bring it to completion (Phil. 1:6). With the Spirit inside us, we live sanctified and are sent preaching the Good News of Jesus daily, not just to ourselves but to those around us also. Paul says it perfectly, "To this end I strenuously contend with all the energy Christ so powerfully works in me" (Col. 1:29 NIV). Sanctification is not a process of trying harder to become like Christ. It is trusting in our new identity that has been given to us in Christ and walking in that identity with the Spirit's help.

This process looks like us walking in the belief that . . .

- We have already been declared righteous. Our good works do not add to or take away from that declaration. Phew. Pressure's off.
- The Holy Spirit is with us, in us, and empowers us in this maturation process. We are not alone in working this thing out.
- We are new creations in Christ. Through the power of the Holy Spirit, we will be transformed more and more into the image of Christ and walk in the good works he has prepared for us (Eph. 2:10).

Friends, this is the new life we've been given in Christ, and it's ours to walk in today. This isn't something where we attain characteristics through external striving and behavior modification; rather, it is life change that happens on the inside over time as we walk in a trust-filled relationship with God. Many of us desire and expect this life change to happen instantaneously, but it is a process that occurs throughout our lifetime. We might want all the changes to happen now and can even shame ourselves for not having arrived yet. Just know, the Lord is so patient with us. He is in us and with us for the long haul. He is committed to us! Are we willing to be patient with ourselves, or are we going to cling to unrealistic expectations and man-made standards?

It all comes down to this: some of us have believed that if we really put our minds and wills to it, we can change into a better version of ourselves. Yet, when we place our confidence to change in our own self effort, we will slowly grow disillusioned and frustrated when we find ourselves stuck in the same old habits. There is a better way. We can choose to believe that our very nature has been changed. We have been declared righteous, and we are slowly becoming what we already are through the power of Christ. We have a new identity. We can place our confidence to change, mature, and grow in our new identity in him. As we grow, he teaches us how to surrender to his design quicker, say yes to refinement, and agree with the Holy Spirit's leading in our lives. We will still have hiccups, slipups, and bad days, but at the end of the day, we go back to our trust in the God who made us and is working everything out.

REFLECT & RESPOND

1. How does this understanding of maturing into who God created you to be relieve you from striving?

2. In what areas of your life are you trying to force change through behavior modification instead of relying on the Spirit to transform you?

Notes

[1] Lynch, Thrall, and McNicol, *The Cure*, 10.

[2] Ferris Jabr, "How Does a Caterpillar Turn into a Butterfly?," *Scientific American*, August 10, 2012, https://www.scientificamerican.com/article/caterpillar-butterfly-metamorphosis-explainer/.

[3] Jabr, "How Does a Caterpillar Turn into a Butterfly?"

[4] "Caterpillar Anatomy," Enchanted Learning, accessed July 9, 2021, https://www.enchantedlearning.com/subjects/butterfly/anatomy/Caterpillar.shtml.

[5] Nathan W. Bingham, "What Is Sanctification?," Ligonier Ministries, June 24, 2013, https://www.ligonier.org/blog/what-sanctification/.

PART TWO

THE FALSE GOSPELS THAT KEEP US STUCK

Jesus alone is our greatest hope. He is our mediator, our righteousness, and the only way we stand in right relationship with the Father. In past centuries and even into our present day, we are presented with temptation to add to this magnificent gospel of grace. But when we do this, we find that the addition to the gospel becomes a sinister distortion of the gospel. These false gospels keep us endlessly striving, performing, and desperately stuck in hopelessness. They warp the nature of God and undermine the sacrifice of Jesus, all under the disguise of godly behavior. Having a clear understanding of the gospel helps us call out these imposters. While there are so many gospel distortions, we're going to dive into four distortions that are sure to keep us stuck in striving and hinder us from living in the freedom Christ paid for us to have.

Chapter Seven

THE DIY GOSPEL

Wide-eyed, I stared into the small, murky bowl with my younger brother chanting in my ear, "Just try it already! Quick! Do it!" I could feel the steam rise and graze my face. The intoxicating smell coming from the bowl beneath my hand enticed my nine-year-old rebellious self to just bite the bullet and experience the thrill of the forbidden substance. But I had to take the leap before my mom came back into the room.

(At this point you're probably thinking, *Good gosh almighty, what kind of toxic, drug-related substance did this poor child have unsupervised access to?*) Calm down, y'all. It was my mom's new paraffin wax spa kit. You know, the tub full of hot wax that you can dip your hands and feet in for a rejuvenating moisture treatment? Scandalous, I know.

As soon as I gathered up enough courage, I plunged my hand into the burning wax, amazed that once I pulled my hand back out, I had created a one-of-a-kind hand cast! I was fascinated. Every time my mom whipped that thing out, I would sneak behind her, dip a different extremity into the pot of paraffin, and add it to the makeshift wax museum in my closet. I was proud of my artistic ingenuity.

Many nights later, the faint hum of the ice cream truck managed to unglue my face from the TV. It was 6:00 on the dot, and the ice cream man was making his rounds through my neighborhood. I screamed at my folks to just please give me money (one more time), and my parents kept yelling back that I'd apparently "spent it all." I scoured through couch cushions, rugs, pillows, and my brother's room with no avail. I had seconds before the truck filled with delectable delicacies made its way to the other neighborhood, and I was not about to deny myself from that SpongeBob Popsicle.

Then, it dawned on me.

"Who needs money when you have a collection of one-of-a-kind wax figurines?" Genius. I raided my closet and picked out some of my most prized paraffin possessions, stuffed them in my shirt, and sprinted like a mad woman down the street. Red faced and out of breath, I finally made my way to the five-foot-tall counter of the ice cream truck. With a huge grin on my face, I looked up and said, "Sir, I have something I would like to offer you." I laid the grubby, half-smashed wax extremities on the counter as this poor man's eyes grew wide. "These are real expensive wax fingers that I think you could use in your business . . . Did I mention they're made of wax? They're even stretchy, so you'll be able to wear them on your fingers for protection. I'm willing to give you all ten fingers . . . for one of those SpongeBobs."

He didn't flinch. (I truly did think he'd be more impressed with my offer!) I spent several minutes trying to convince this man that his fingers wouldn't get cold anymore, he wouldn't get sticky fingers from the ice cream . . . the list goes on. He just kept explaining to me over and over, "Honey, I can't trade you because that's not enough. I need actual money."

Deflated, I walked away with no SpongeBob popsicle and a shirt full of wax fingers that just lost a whole lot of value.

I think back to this story often, and I just have to laugh at my incredibly confident and creative entrepreneurial spirit. While that "waxy" form of DIY currency may not have been enough for the ice cream guy, over the years I started to learn all the different forms of social currency people use to get what they want. And unlike the ice cream fiasco, these types of transactions were both reciprocal and successful. It didn't take long to understand that I could curate a desirable self-made currency and exchange it to get what I wanted from other people. What did I want from other people? The affirmation that I was enough and what I had to offer was enough.

I found that a charming personality could gain applause and approval from others, taking on extra work could earn the favor of my authorities, morphing my personality and compromising my own values could help me be liked, and saying yes to every volunteer or ministry opportunity could be exchanged for a sense of feeling . . . good enough. When I felt down, I reminded myself where my worth came from—my work. Deep down, I believed I had done all the right things, carried out the right life decisions, respected the right people, and even loved God in the right ways.

Our "Do It Yourself" Culture

Now some might object and say, "I don't think it's a problem to feel like you are enough or worthy of something." I would agree. However, if the foundation of our satisfaction and worth is not centered on the work of Jesus Christ, we will find ourselves trapped in perpetual cycles of self-inflation, self-promotion, and even self-righteousness. This is difficult because striving to be "good enough" is not something we condemn in our culture—at all. In fact, it's something we encourage and instill in one another.

We train ourselves through positive self-talk to take inventory of the things we've accomplished, the behaviors we've polished, the milestones we've conquered, and the impact we've made on others. We subconsciously tally up in our hearts the good things we've done. Then we use all these things as affirmations; and after consideration, we take a deep breath and offer ourselves this quiet relief: "Phew, I am good enough."

Not surprisingly, many of us, especially those of us in the church, can transfer this same pattern of thinking to our theology. Because we have this inherent desire to be good enough, we can easily (and unknowingly) carry over that desire into our relationship with God. We can find ourselves quietly taking tally of

- Quiet times we have taken
- Verses we've memorized
- People we've witnessed to
- People we've discipled
- Time we've spent praying
- Hours we've spent in church
- Ministries we are actively involved in

The list goes on.

Now these disciplines and activities aren't things we are publicly bragging about. No, these are things we are mentally checking off when we start to feel insecure in our relationship with God—when we wonder if we're still good enough for him. When we start to question, "Am I in good standing with God?" this becomes the list many of us flip through to assure ourselves that we are. At least, this has been the case for me.

I don't know about you, but for much of my relationship with Christ, I felt uncertain about my standing with God. It was like I was always trying not to make him mad at me. When my life and outward behavior didn't feel "put together," and I wasn't checking off the spiritual checkboxes I thought I should, I assumed God loved me less and would even use me less. My relationship with God and salvation felt like it hung in the balance of my behavior. In my mind, salvation was dependent on my actions, my good behavior, and my one-sided ability to keep God happy with me. The driving force behind this kind of lifestyle is not a new one. In fact, it has been threatening the church and its followers for centuries. These beliefs all come in line behind a gospel distortion I like to call the DIY Gospel.

The "Do-It-Yourself" Gospel

The heart of this false gospel ultimately proclaims that the righteousness I bring to the table is enough, and I have no need for the righteousness of Christ. Ouch. We would likely never confess these words in the middle of our Wednesday night small group, but our actions and lives can make these words a banner we unknowingly live by. When we believe our own works can contribute to or take away from the work of Christ on the cross, we have fallen into the systems of a different gospel.

There is a parable embedded in the book of Matthew that has always been one that, frankly, frustrated me. Months ago, I read this parable for the umpteenth time and finally had the nerve to shut my Bible and say, "Lord, this is kind of rude of you to say."

You can find the story in Matthew 22:1–14. The backdrop of this story takes place with Jesus telling multiple parables amid a few pompous Pharisees who were hanging on to every word Jesus said. Not because his words gave them life, but because they were looking for words that would give them grounds to take his life. Jesus sets the stage of his teaching by saying the kingdom of God is like a king who was throwing a wedding feast for his beloved son. At first, he sent an initial invitation to a certain group of people who said they didn't want to attend. The king sent more servants to invite this same sect of people and still they declined. Finally, the king gave orders to the servants to invite anyone and everyone they could—both good and evil—to come and enjoy the banquet for his son. This time, the banquet was filled with guests. Now, this is the part that got me all out of sorts:

> When the king came in to see the guests, he saw a man there who was not dressed for a wedding. So he said to him, "Friend, how did you get in here without wedding clothes?" The man was speechless. Then the king told the attendants, "Tie him up hand and foot, and throw him into the outer darkness, where there will be weeping and gnashing of teeth." (Matt. 22:11–14)

These were my three combative points I made clear to the Lord that night:

1. The king invited all people, including the poor, to his banquet in the story. Of course they didn't have the right attire! Sheesh.
2. Why couldn't the man just wear his clothes? Why was the king so picky?
3. What exactly is the right kind of wedding attire for a celebration like this?

Despite my frustration with this passage, I decided to do a little bit of research on Jewish wedding customs.

When we read the Bible, it's very important to consider cultural and historical context to understand the message trying to be conveyed. To my surprise, I learned that it was custom in ancient Jewish culture for the wedding host, especially a king, to provide wedding garments for the guests to wear. According to John Reid, "These wedding garments were simple, nondescript robes that all attendees wore. In this way, rank or station was covered, so everyone at the feast could mingle as equals."[1] We see a similar provision of garments in Genesis 45:22 when Pharoah prompts Joseph to provide a change of clothing for his brothers before they entered Pharaoh's presence. This puts our underdressed fella here in an entirely different predicament. It wasn't that he didn't have proper wedding clothes that got him thrown out; it was because he refused the garments the king provided for him. We can't be sure why he refused them. Perhaps he thought his own clothes were good enough. Or maybe he wasn't brave enough to let his old garments go and accept a grandiose gift of a wedding garment.

Now, when Jesus told parables, he typically used a fictional story to describe a kingdom reality. This parable reveals to us that in the Kingdom of God, there is a certain attire we must have—a certain covering that is needed to dine and dwell in the presence of God. The harsh truth? Our DIY outfit crafted from our own good works, untouchable reputation, and self-righteous resume won't cut it. We are not enough, in and of ourselves, to bridge the gap between ourselves and the Father. There is only one man who can allow us to do that, and we need his covering.

Confident in the Covering

> *"Therefore, since we have been justified by faith, we have peace with God through our Lord Jesus Christ. We have also obtained access through him by faith into this grace in which we stand, and we boast in the hope of the glory of God."* —Romans 5:1–2

When we accept this gift of grace that God offers us through his Son Jesus, we are justified, as we discussed a few chapters ago. This word in the Greek is *dikaioō*, which means to "render righteous" or "such as he ought to be."[2]

As he ought to be.

This brings me back to the imagery of God, man, and woman in the garden of Eden.

No sin.

No shame.

No separation.

No need for a covering.

Just nightly walks, unhindered intimacy—life as it ought to be.

But it was that one choice, the one bite of forbidden fruit, that undid and warped all that ought to be. Because now the people who inhabited the world were unable to stop sinning.

Ridden with shame.

Separated spiritually from their Maker.

In desperate need of a permanent covering.

That is where we find ourselves without a Savior. There is no amount of building, striving, award winning, and God pleasing that we can do to make things as they ought to be. But at the moment of our salvation, when we trust in the life, death, resurrection, and sufficiency of God's Son Jesus, we become justified—our soul is made right and acceptable by God. God takes the righteousness and perfection of his Son and clothes the believer in a perfect robe. With this covering, robed in the pure righteousness of Jesus Christ, we can dwell and dine in the presence of God.

When we are convinced that our good behavior can somehow "woo" God into waiving our sin, we are mistaken and misled. When we get caught up in these cycles of trying to earn our way into God's kingdom, it's almost like we are trying to pay our way into his presence with grubby wax fingers. We are just like the man at the wedding feast who showed up in his own possessions, rejecting the gift of the King in hopes that what he brought in his own effort would be enough. It was not enough then, and it is not enough now. Where there is no robe, there is no relationship because there is no righteousness. We cannot do this thing without Jesus.

Our DIY wedding outfit just ain't gonna cut it.

Becoming versus Striving

Maybe you have a story like mine: you grew up in the church, you have followed all the rules, and you have striven to do all the "right things." When this is our story, it can be difficult for us to remember that just like everyone else, we must be born again. At the moment of our salvation, we were given a completely new identity and nature.

In his conversation with Nicodemus in John 3:3, Jesus tells Nicodemus that unless someone is born again, they cannot see the kingdom of God. If this is the case, the goal of our Christian life is not to keep our old nature and continue striving in hopes that someday it will be godly enough. The goal isn't to try and bedazzle our sin-soaked robe, hoping it will somehow be enough to stand before the presence of God. We must be reborn into a new nature. This rebirthing process looks like becoming a baby with many—many—immature behaviors. But the Holy Spirit, Christ, and God are now fused within our nature. Their divine influence on our soul turns us to Christ, keeps us, strengthens us, increases our belief, and fans in us the flame to walk out the very heart of God. All that is enough is now in us and with us.

So you know what? We can stop trying so dang hard.

We can stop trying to jump through hoops of holy hustle and walking tightropes trying to please a God who has already fully justified us in Christ. It's amazing—the more we trust in the sufficiency of his work on the cross and his work in us, the more we will find ourselves walking in the good works he's called us to do. We now realize we aren't doing good things to be accepted; out of the overflow of God's kindness toward us, we carry out good works because we know we already are accepted.

Friends, we can retire the old, cheaply bedazzled robe we used to believe was enough. Instead, we can walk in confidence as we allow ourselves to be adorned with a better robe—the robe of righteousness, which was bought with the precious blood of Jesus.

REFLECT & RESPOND

1. Can you think of any thoughts, beliefs, or behaviors you are currently walking in that fall into the trap of the false, DIY Gospel?

2. How does the reality that you are adorned with Christ's perfect robe of righteousness change the way you approach God?

Notes

[1] John O. Reid, "Many Are Called, Few Are Chosen," Bible Tools, *Forerunner*, March–April 2016, https://www.bibletools.org/index.cfm/fuseaction/Library.sr/CT/RA/k/1703/many-are-called-few-are-chosen.htm.

[2] "Lexicon :: Strong's G1344 – *dikaioō*," Blue Letter Bible, accessed July 12, 2021, https://www.blueletterbible.org/lexicon/g1344/kjv/tr/0-1/.

Chapter Eight

THE "SO THAT" GOSPEL

Unmet expectations or disappointment will often lead us to question, deconstruct, or even cash in on a belief we hold about God. Because when the ground beneath our feet starts to shake, it forces us to assess the security of the foundation on which we've built our beliefs.

For me, that questioning was slow going but eventually reached a boiling point a year ago when I glanced down at the umpteenth stick that once again reminded me of the same disappointing news: you are not pregnant. It wasn't really a big deal at first—I tend to be pretty easy going. But then one month turned into two, then four, then eight, and then a dozen more of hoping and being let down at the same disheartening reality. Months of disappointment finally broke my filter and my heart. I did not hold back when I let out the bitterness that had been brewing in my soul. Sad sobs quickly turned into angry accusations laid out before the throne of God.

I've been good, God. This whole time, I've tried to be a "good Christian girl" who waited. That's what you wanted, right? I read all the books. I got the dang purity ring. I was very careful. I played by the rules. And now I'm infuriated because **I did** all these things **so that** you would bless my future family. That's what I was promised. Yet here I am—still not pregnant.

And there it was—the belief that fueled my bitterness all the more: I did _____ **so that** God would _____.

Well, I'm here to tell you—God made no such promises to bless my womb if I did x, y, and z. (Purity culture did, but that's a soap box for another day.)

When that statement fell out of my mouth, I knew it wasn't true, but it didn't help that I still believed it. Yet in that moment, it made me ask myself what else I believed God would do for me as a reward for my "hard work." One by one, I confessed things:

- I've been involved in ministry **so that** God will be impressed by my service to him and reward me.
- I exercise and try to eat right **so that** God will see my diligence and bless my health.
- I tithe **so that** God will bless me with material abundance.
- I make time for prayer, fasting, and Bible study **so that** God will honor my consistency and answer my prayers.

And as I asked my friends, I learned that I wasn't the only one struggling with these distorted beliefs. They too, mentioned things:

- I go to church **so that** God won't be disappointed with me.
- I obey what God says **so that** he won't punish me through adversity.

- I read my Bible everyday **so that** I will feel okay and not experience anxiety or depression.
- I make the right choices **so that** I won't experience brokenness or have bad things happen to me.
- I married the right person **so that** God would bless my marriage and give me smooth sailing.

In each of these scenarios, you'll notice a positive moral input equals a positive outcome. Each phrase hangs on the belief that if we live a good, moral life, then we should be blessed with a good life in return. Whether we've been believers for forever or for just a little while, we can easily fall into the narratives of yet another distorted gospel I like to call the "So That" Gospel.

When it comes down to it, this "gospel" proclaims the good news that a person can find security in their moralistic sacrifices because they believe God will repay them by shielding them from suffering or discomfort.

Out of all the false gospels we will talk about in this book, I believe this one holds the greatest capacity for painful disillusionment, a great falling away, and a rejection of Christianity altogether in many lives. Because when life gets hard, when circumstances take an unexpected turn and things don't play out like we thought, our distorted belief about God can lead us to conclude that **he has utterly failed us, that he is not trustworthy, and he certainly isn't kind.**

A Formulaic Faith

When we boil this gospel down, we will find a formulaic relationship that operates on an input/output system. It is anchored in the belief that when we fill our lives with and input good things, good behaviors, and good habits, God will bless us with good outcomes and comfortable circumstances—not those of suffering, hardship, or struggle.

I do want to pause here and say that there are natural good consequences in life that are a direct result of wise choices. The book of Proverbs is full of examples! Spiritually, when we pursue making healthy, wise choices, we avoid self-inflicted heartbreak, destruction, and consequences that come from folly. There are tangible rewards that God addresses in Scripture for following his commands and instruction—because he designed it that way! Not to mention, at the end of our lives, we will give an account and be repaid for the things we've done in our bodies, good or bad (2 Cor. 5:10)! Physically, when it comes to health and wellness, when we eat right and exercise, our bodies typically become healthier. If we are managing our money wisely, most of the time, we have more to steward. When we spend time in God's Word, we do experience peace and growth because God's Word is life giving and life changing! I'm not saying that it is wrong to pursue health, managed finances, healthy spiritual disciplines, or that there aren't any rewards for godly living. These are all good things that we *should* steward well!

But when we take these good and godly things and turn them into a list of reasons why God should repay us with blessing for all the "hard work" we've done, that's where we've breached gospel parameters and are no longer operating in truth. Not only does this mentality treat our heavenly Father like a vending machine, but it can lead us to conclude that suffering, hardship, or trial is somehow a punishment from God or a direct result of not working hard enough.

At the heart of the real gospel, we see Jesus—the God man—who left the glory of heaven for the grime of a fallen earth. He didn't use his equality with God to his advantage (Phil. 2:6) but rather came to bow low and serve the people who would eventually nail him to a cross. Jesus, the dearly beloved Son of God, did not model for us a life without struggle, disappointment, or adversity. He modeled that even in his perfection and sinless state, suffering would be part of his life. In fact, he literally told people that if they were going to be his followers, they should go ahead and anticipate trouble and hardship.[1]

As much as we might want to, we cannot rewrite suffering out of our stories—but that is exactly what the "So That" Gospel convinces us we can do through hard work and moral sacrifice. The outrageous thing is that, historically, Satan has tried to lead people astray using a very similar narrative to the "So That" Gospel. And out of all the people he attempted to convince, guess who he went after?

Jesus.

A Story without Suffering

Matthew chapter four sets the scene for a showdown between Jesus and the enemy. Jesus had been fasting for forty days and forty nights, so when he was approached by Satan, he was tired, weak, and hungry. Three different times during their discourse, Satan questioned Jesus's sonship to the Father by presenting multiple requests and scenarios. Each time, Jesus refused and refuted his requests with Scripture.

The first time he tempted Jesus, he tested him by telling him to prove his sonship by turning stones on the ground into bread. Jesus responded by saying, "Man must not live on bread alone but on every word that comes from the mouth of God" (Matt. 4:4). The second time, he took him up to the top of the temple that overlooked the city and told him to throw himself down off the building because Scripture said that the angels would support him and keep him safe. Once again, Jesus responded with Scripture, saying, "Do not test the Lord your God" (Matt. 4:7). Finally, Satan took him to the top of a tall mountain that overlooked all the kingdoms of the world and told Jesus that if he would bow down and worship him, he would give Jesus all of it. At that, Jesus commanded Satan to go away and left him with one final word: "Worship the Lord your God, and serve only him" (Matt. 4:10).

The same tempter who struck the vulnerable places in Adam and Eve and shoots lies straight to our vulnerable places took a stab at the Son of God, aiming straight for the places in which he thought he could gain territory or a foothold. This passage left me wondering, "Of all the places Satan could prod, what area would he target? Of all the things he could dangle in Jesus's face, what reality might be the most enticing to him?"

Phillip Yancey hits the nail on the head when he concludes that Satan "tempted Jesus toward the good parts of being human without the bad: to savor the taste of bread without being subject to the fixed rules of hunger and of agriculture, to confront risk with no real danger, to enjoy fame and power without the prospect of painful rejection—in short, to wear a crown but not a cross."[2]

Imagine that—a life without suffering. This same temptation to write out suffering would arise multiple times from the mouths of many different people during Jesus's ministry. One of those temptations came from the mouth of one of his disciples, Peter, who rebuked Jesus when he told him the Son of Man would have to suffer and die. At that moment, Jesus looked at Peter and said, "Get behind me, Satan! You are a stumbling block to me; you do not have in mind the concerns of God, but merely human concerns" (Matt. 16:21–23 NIV). Even as he hung on a cross, the people hurled insults at him: "You saved others—now save yourself. . . . Aren't you the Messiah? Save yourself and us . . . if you are really the king of Jews—rescue yourself!"

Jesus could have done all those things, but he didn't. In all reality, he could have demolished Satan in the desert that day with the flick of his wrist, sparing an entire people group from a life of living with an accuser. He could have come to put his foot down in kingly power and establish earthly justice, just like the people of Israel wanted. He could have modeled a life to his disciples of superseding suffering instead of succumbing to it. At any time, he could have overridden the laws of nature, the power of man, and even compelled the belief in stubborn hearts. So why did Jesus exercise restraint? Why does God restrain, even today?

As Yancey says, this could be because, perhaps,

> God's terrible insistence on human freedom is so absolute that he granted us the power to live as though he did not exist, to spit in his face, to crucify him.... God insists on such restraint because no pyrotechnic displays of omnipotence will achieve the response he desires. Although power can force obedience, only love can summon a response of love, which is the one thing God wants from us and the reason he created us.[3]

Removing the power to choose from people produces a merely coercive response. God's design wasn't to multiply robots, forced and obligated to follow him. He wants children who respond to his overwhelming and all-encompassing love for us. We love because he loved us first (1 John 4:19). We love out of being totally filled by him.

Living Beloved and Living "Because"

The "So That" gospel will ultimately produce fearful, distant, and duty-oriented employees banking on a raise for their hard work. It is yet another narrative that traps us in a hamster wheel of striving because we're trying to collect enough "good" inputs to prevent a not-so-good outcome. Yet, when hardship comes, the person who has been trying hard to live up to different moral standards is either going to be angry with God because he isn't repaying them for their hard work or they are going to feel incredible anger toward themselves, because it must mean they aren't doing enough. Tim Keller states, "If evil circumstances overtake you, and you are not sure whether your life has been good enough or not, you may swing miserably back and forth between the poles of 'I hate Thee!' and 'I hate me.'"[4]

Operating out of a mindset of duty, fear, or selfish expectation is not the way God wants to be loved by us. I mean, can we blame him? Is this the kind of love we desire? No! Our hearts would break a million times over to hear that our friends or children only love us because they are simply afraid of us, they feel like they are obligated to, or because they're trying to butter us up to get something later. We were created in the image of the God of love, who by very nature is love and desires love from his kids.

The real gospel reminds us that we are children of the living God, the objects of his love and affection. Out of our satisfied, secure, and trust-filled relationship with him, we are free to operate in our position as ambassadors of Christ who are commissioned and sent, living fiercely free because of the love we've received from God. We don't sprint for kudos. We sprint because we are in this for kingdom come, eternally secured in Christ and in the power of the Spirit who keeps, equips, and empowers us.

While we have been given new life on the inside, we are still temporary inhabitants of a fallen world, where suffering is part of the gig no matter how "good" we are. It rains and shines "on the just and on the unjust" (Matt. 5:45 ESV). But the difference is our hope is not found in this world. Our hope is in our home to come, in the heavenly abode that waits for our return. In that glorious place, there is no suffering, and the presence of God is the only thing that has our gaze. But until that day, we live here below as the beloved of God, demonstrating and telling of this life-changing love to the world around us. But make no mistake—this doesn't excuse us into a life of simply sitting until Jesus comes back. It will not be a pony ride. We have work to do. We will wage war against demonic strongholds and devices that set themselves up against what God is doing. Our lives as Christ-followers are a response to a call to pick up our cross and die to ourselves daily. Our faith in what Christ has done will show itself through our actions and works (James 2:18).

HOWEVER.

We don't walk in these things **so that** God will love us, bless us, give something to us, or shield us from suffering.

No.

We live sent, commissioned into the good works he has planned for us **because . . .**

- We are fully accepted by God in Christ, declared righteous. We have nothing to prove to him.
- We are infinitely, immeasurably, and undeniably loved by God right where we are.
- We are in process, being transformed more and more into the image of Christ.
- God is good, he does good, and he is for our good. He will never stop being good.
- He is the giver of all good and perfect gifts. His heart for us is kind.
- We have a hope that can never be taken away.
- We have help in the Holy Spirit who is our teacher and guide, and who sustains us in times of hardship.
- We trust his love for us.
- We love him.

The gospel gives us the freedom to do good things not so that God will somehow act on our behalf, but because God has already acted on our behalf, allowing us to run secure in his love and goodness. Changing our perspective from "so that" to "because" completely changes our narratives; we now live with a completely new way of thinking.

- We spend time in God's Word and in prayer **because** Christ has brought us to life and we want to connect with him and learn from him.
- We get plugged into ministry and service **because** Christ has changed our hearts and we want to build up other believers' hearts.
- We are on the lookout for ways to love others through good works **because** Christ has loved us and we want people to see God and his transformative love through our actions.
- We share the gospel with others **because** Christ has empowered us through the Spirit to carry this message. We want people to know Jesus, enjoy him, and walk with him forever.

So I ask you today: What are your "so thats"? If you were to take a hard look at the things you believe about God and even the disappointments you have encountered in your life, are there things you are doing because you believe God will give you a certain outcome if you achieve them? Take some time to write down these "so thats"; and as we journey together, slowly pair those with a "because."

As Louie Giglio says in his teaching "Rejection Must Fall,"[5] when we live from a place of "so that," we are ultimately living **for** acceptance. But when we live from a place of "because," we are living **from** already being accepted. The good news explicitly states that we are accepted by God when we put our trust and faith in Christ and surrender our lives to him. He is our justification, our acceptance, our enough. My friends, this completely changes the way we live, the way we love, and the way we serve. It is freedom, and it is yours for the taking today **because** Christ has already done and won it all. For you. For us. For the world.

REFLECT & RESPOND

1. Take a hard look at some of your life's greatest disappointments, discouragements, or even uncertainties. Are there any areas of your life in which you have formed the belief that you have to do _____ so that God will _____? Write some of those things down and bring them to the light.

2. There is a difference between living our lives **for** God's acceptance and living **from** a place of already being accepted by God. How would your life look different if you chose to believe the latter? What things would you be free to do?

Notes

[1] See Scriptures such as John 16:33, Matthew 10:22, and 1 Peter 4:12.

[2] Philip Yancey, "Temptation: Showdown in the Desert," in *The Jesus I Never Knew* (Grand Rapids: Zondervan, 2002), 72.

[3] Yancey, "Temptation," 78.

[4] Timothy Keller, "Redefining Lostness," in *The Prodigal God: Recovering the Heart of the Christian Faith* (New York: Penguin Books, 2016), 57.

[5] Louie Giglio, "Goliath Must Fall - Session 3," *Vimeo*, accessed July 12, 2021, https://vimeo.com/258782126.

Chapter Nine

THE GOSPEL OF GRIT

"Just do your best and let God do the rest."

This phrase is plastered on Christian tees, painted on coffee mugs, and it's the classic slogan parents tell their kids before taking a big test. I can't tell you how many times I've told somebody this when they were nervous, unsure, or in the midst of a big decision.

While I don't think this phrase is inherently wrong or heretical, it does paint an interesting picture of our relationship with God. Being a visual person by nature, when I hear this phrase and those like it, I picture a relay race. In this race, I am the first one to run. With my best foot forward, I will run as fast as I can, but once I get tired of running and am ready to tap out, I'll hand the baton to God for him to finish and do what he does best. God will do his part, and I will do mine.

The main problem I find with this phrase is the conjunction. (Grammar refresher: a conjunction is a word that adds two entities together.) Do your best *and* let God do the rest. It creates this hypothetical equation in which my effort plus Christ's sufficiency equals success. We are a team, Christ *and* me. When we find ourselves with a "Christ *and* me" relationship, we will often think things like this:

- God has paid the ultimate sacrifice, given me his word, and placed me on a solid foundation; now it's my job to carry out the good works he's planned for me.
- God did all the work to bring me to him; now it's up to me to live for him.
- I'll use the strength I have to power through, and when I tap out, God will step in.
- God has supplied me with truth to know better; now I must be and do better.

With this view, Christ is portrayed as the outside energy source we run to for fuel, and the one we cry out to when we're out. Like battery-powered energizer bunnies, we fuel up on the things of God, and then we run, run, run. But inevitably when our batteries run out and die, we experience shame, exhaustion, and overall burnout. We cry out for God's rescue and are refueled, but then we enter back into the same cycle all over again: fuel up, run fast, grow exhausted, burn out. But perhaps the most dangerous logic this thinking can lead to is believing God did his part through justification and making us right with him, and now it's on us to carry out the work of maturing and growing in Christ through sanctification.

When it comes down to it, this mentality of "Christ *and* me" places more emphasis on my own grit than on the continual empowerment of the Holy Spirit through grace. A Christ *and* me relationship is at the center of a gospel distortion I call the Gospel of Grit, which is really no gospel at all. While it acknowledges Christ's sufficient work on the cross, it demands that we carry out the implications of that freedom by ourselves. It preaches that it is our job to sanctify ourselves through effort. As a result, it keeps us stuck in a cycle of trying hard while we grow increasingly frustrated and bitter with our own inability to change and sanctify ourselves through willpower. Thankfully, God has given us an unfathomable gift through the gospel. A gift that remained a mystery for centuries but has now been fully revealed to us in Christ (Col. 1:26). This mystery makes all the difference in our lives. Paul will tell us how.

The Mystery Revealed

In his letter to the church at Colossae, Paul wrote not only to encourage the believers, but also to combat heretical false teachings that sought to add to or take away from the gospel they had been told. While it is tough to nail down the exact heresy that was floating around, Paul gives us little clues as to what these false teachings entailed. In Colossians 2, Paul warns the believers not to let others judge them for what they eat, drink, or whether they participate in different observances. He went on to say these false teachers take pride in their ascetic practices, self-made religion, fake humility, and harsh treatment of their bodies.

Ascetic practices are ultimately rooted in a type of doctrine known as asceticism. According to Merriam-Webster, "asceticism" is defined as "the practice of strict self-denial as a measure of personal and especially spiritual discipline."[1] In other words, it hinges on the belief that through a person's own will power, they can attain a new level of spirituality or righteousness by strenuous, self-driven effort. These practices centered around rules that called for abstaining from natural things so a person could live a more righteous, moral life with a higher level of connection with God. Without a doubt, these practices would lead to a pride-inflated heart that believed one's own betterment was sheerly because of personal ability.

Paul rejected this kind of thinking, arguing that while this type of fleshly restraint has a reputation for wisdom, when it came down to it, these harsh practices actually held no value in curbing self-indulgence (Col. 2:23). Asceticism gives the appearance of having the power to absolve the flesh while operating completely out of fleshly desire and control. It has no power! While we may not have people flooding our churches trying to convince us into an ascetic lifestyle like in the Colossian church, the Gospel of Grit fits right along these lines because it too relies on a form of self-effort to attain godliness and deny the flesh. It promotes a "Christ *and* me" type of thinking—Christ did his part, and now it's time for me to do mine. And that is why Paul had good news for the people of the Colossian church, and he has good news for us, too.

After the introduction of his letter, Paul starts alluding to this mystery that he must reveal to them (Col. 1:26). I can see the audience skimming this letter out of anticipation, trying to find this hidden mystery. Finally, Paul lets them in on the secret: "God wanted to make known among the Gentiles the glorious wealth of this mystery, which is Christ in you, the hope of glory" (Col. 1:27). Oh, my friends, these three words—*Christ in you*—are life-giving freedom. Who knew one little preposition could change absolutely everything? (Grammar refresher: prepositions tell the position of something.)

The Power of a Preposition

The good news for the Colossian church that day was that they no longer had to put their trust in external, fleshly practices to attain holiness and spiritual growth. No, no. These words reminded them that the power to change, mature, and grow was not fueled by what they could do but because of who was in them. The power is in the preposition: *in*. Come on, say that out loud: The power is in the preposition!

The Gospel of Grit paints Christ as merely **additional**—after he's done the work, we're left to do the work on our own, and he's there for us to run to when we need him. The promise of this distorted gospel is that we can change, grow, and mature through self-determination. But this process has left so many believers frustrated, stuck, and exhausted because our flesh can only take us so far. We will eventually come to the conclusion that we cannot do what God is asking us to do. We can't keep this up. The truth is: we can't! We cannot live a life of walking in the Spirit while trying to do it through our flesh (Gal. 5:16). There is a better way. The real gospel, the gospel of Jesus, introduces us to the groundbreaking reality that our relationship with Christ is not additional; it's **prepositional.** There are so many other prepositions God could have chosen to represent our relationship with Christ. It could have been Christ *around* me, Christ *above* me, Christ *outside* me, or even Christ *near* me. But instead, he chose the most intimate position of relationship: **Christ *in* me.** He is not an outside force; he is an inside source. Instead of operating like a battery-powered energizer bunny, we live instead by abiding in him, being connected to a source that is never going to run out. His very essence, Spirit, and power are placed in the interior of our hearts, not to act as a supplement to our own strength but to be the substance of it (Col. 2:17). Christ *and* me portrays two entities—Christ *in* me paints a fused union.

Later in Paul's letter, he expounds on this truth by saying, "For the entire fullness of God's nature dwells bodily in Christ, and you have been filled by him, who is the head over every ruler and authority" (Col. 2:9–10). The fullness of Christ in you, friend. I love that he didn't just save us, forgive us, and then kick us out of the nest to try and fly on our own. Instead, he placed his very Spirit—the Holy Spirit—inside of our being to be the substance of our renewal, the catalyst that transforms us day by day into the image of our creator (Col. 3:10). Every single thing we need, we have in Christ, who is *in* us.

When I feel powerless against temptation: Christ *in* me gives me strength.

When the hurt is real and I want to use my words as a weapon: Christ *in* me teaches me how to walk in love.

When I'm trembling, afraid, and lack confidence: Christ *in* me is my confidence.

When I feel beat up by the lies of the enemy: Christ *in* me convinces my heart of truth.

When fear cripples me into the fetal position: Christ *in* me stands up and gives me courage.

When I am incapable of changing: Christ *in* me changes my heart and gives me new desires.

When despair and disappointment take my breath away, I remember: Christ *in* me is the hope of glory.

In his Bible study on Colossians, Louie Giglio gives a wonderful revelation the Lord impressed on his heart about this freedom from Christ *and* me to Christ *in* me. He paints this picture of Jesus saying, "I not only did all the work to bring you *to* God, but I'm living in you to supply the power to allow you to walk *in* God."[2] We are empowered, equipped, and sent because of who is in us. But my friends, this mystery doesn't mean we simply lean back and say, "Meh. Jesus will fix all that. He can make what he wants to happen, happen. He can move me if he wants to. If he's already done all the work, there's nothing for me to do!" This is not the case. Grace is not the couch we kick back and sit on; it becomes the track we run on. As Dallas Willard says, "Grace . . . is the fuel that propels us forward."[3] We are not called to a life of lay down and relax; we are called to a life of lean and run. However, we are not called to run this thing alone.

More than Just Me

Often in the New Testament, when the word "you" is used to address people (like in the phrase "Christ in you"), the word is not singular, it is plural. In English we don't have a common word to communicate the plural form of the word "you"; but lucky for us, we do have a plural word for "you" in Texan: ***y'all***. When Paul is addressing the believers in this letter, he isn't just revealing to them that Christ is in you individually, but that as believers, Christ is in us, collectively. He is essentially saying, "This is the mystery: Christ in y'all." Our identity in Christ is not as privatized, individual people. Rather, we are found *in* Christ as a corporate group of sons and daughters: the body of Christ.

While it is important for us to recognize the importance of Christ's inhabitation in our own hearts, it is even more powerful to recognize that his very life, breath, and Spirit are in the believers around us. It is not just Christ empowering me to walk in God; he is empowering us all collectively, binding us together in love. As Spirit-infused people, we can experience Christ through one another. Just as we can give grace to others because Christ is in us, we can receive grace from other people because Christ is in them, too. When we are depleted, checked out, and void of strength, Christ in others can encourage our hearts, be the hands and feet of the Savior, and nourish our tired souls. Christ empowers us not only through his presence inside of us, but also through his Spirit in other people. When we align our lives to this "gospel of grit," we ultimately find our identity in being an individual entity, with ourselves as the main power source. Yet, when we align our lives with the true gospel, we find that our identities become deeply rooted in divine community—dependent on Christ and one another. We aren't solo runners, training for our own health. We run in his strength together.

Striving with His Strength

After Paul reveals the mystery of "Christ in us" to the Colossian believers, he doesn't stop there. This mystery is just the *how* to do what God has called us to. He goes on to say,

> So we tell others about Christ, warning everyone and teaching everyone with all the wisdom God has given us. We want to present them to God, perfect in their relationship to Christ. That's why I work and struggle so hard, depending on Christ's mighty power that works within me. (Col. 1:28–29 NLT)

Paul says that in light of this new reality of having Christ inside us—in that hope—we go.

We run.
We tell people about Jesus.
We invest in other's lives.
We plan.
We teach.
We work hard.
We lay our lives down.
We love even when it hurts.
We use our gifts.
We scatter seeds like crazy people.
We make this life count.
We keep our eyes on the Kingdom while our prayer is to see it come *here*.

Yet in doing all these things, we remember this reality: Christ *in* us. But as Paul says, while he is running and working hard that people may know Christ, he is leaning on Christ's power. He is running and relying at the exact same time. I love how the Christian Standard Bible translates this last verse: "I labor for this,

striving with his strength that works powerfully in me (Col. 1:29—emphasis mine).

Wait—**striving?** No! Aren't we freed from a life of striving?

Here's the beauty, friends. When we understand our new life in Christ—the finality of what he's done, the new nature he's bestowed upon us, and his placement of the Spirit in us—**he redirects our striving.** Because now we aren't striving for, we're striving from. Alas! The power is—yet again—in the preposition! We aren't striving *for* his acceptance, *for* higher spirituality, or *for* a maturity earned by self-will. We strive *from* a place of acceptance, knowing we are declared right before God, secure in his love, and empowered with his Spirit who is our substance, our inner strength—now until we go home. He is not the coach on the sideline barking orders he cannot fulfill himself. He is the coach on the inside, giving us the power, the desire, and the ability to do what he has called us to do. And he is fully capable of fulfilling everything he is asking us to do. With that knowledge—we run.

Living a Life of Lean

Therefore, this process of transformation—of sanctification—isn't a passive experience on our part. It's an empowered experience. Jesus is the inspiration and conviction. He reveals sinful, immature behaviors that are not a reflection of him. He highlights areas of wrong belief about him, ourselves, and others. He is the voice of wisdom leading us in decisions. He places people in our lives to both sharpen and be sharpened by. He provides us with community to grow in our knowledge of him and his body. He is the catalyst, but we've gotta move our feet, yield to his spirit, and surrender—again and again. As he reveals those caverns in our hearts to which we refuse to give him access, through trust in him, we give him the keys. This transformation is fueled by trust in him, in who he is, and whom he has made us to be.

Yet there will be times when we come to a place where we feel like we can't do the things he's placed before us.

Times when we love the thing he's asked us to surrender, and we don't want to.

Times when we don't want to give him access.

Times when we don't believe what he's spoken about himself and about us.

And in those times, we can confess our unbelief (Mark 9:24), and he will meet us there. It's okay to be honest—to confess that we can't do it; that we can't muster it up. We can ask and allow him to change the desire itself that we may walk in belief of what is true. He is the substance of our lives, our ever-present help, the anchor in which we trust, and our glorious inheritance.

Friend, as you are running, you can guarantee that you will come up against the temptation to try and do this thing yourself. To strap up your boots and grit your way through fear, rejection, insecurity, and struggle. In those moments, pause and get quiet. Quiet enough to hear your new heartbeat. The heartbeat that reminds you that this isn't something you have to do on your own. Put your hand over your heart and feel the pulse. Let your ears hear its anthem. With every beat, let it serve as a loud, tangible reminder of how you will walk the rest of this life out:

CHRIST
      IN
           ME

CHRIST
      IN
           YOU

CHRIST
      IN
           US

REFLECT & RESPOND

1. When we hold the viewpoint that our relationship with Jesus is Christ *and* me, we tend to believe that Christ did his part and now we must do the rest. How have you seen this play out in your life?

2. Our relationship with Jesus is not Christ *and* me but Christ *in* me. Check out these synonyms for the word "in": within, in the middle of, inside, in the interior of. How does the assurance that Christ is within you give you confidence to walk in the things to which he's called you?

Notes

[1] *Merriam-Webster.com Dictionary*, s.v. "asceticism," accessed July 13, 2021, https://www.merriam-webster.com/dictionary/asceticism.

[2] Louie Giglio, "The Book of Colossians," RightNow Media, accessed July 13, 2021, https://www.rightnowmedia.org/Content/Series/287526?episode=3.

[3] Dallas Willard, K. Harney, and S. Harney, *The Divine Conspiracy Participant's Guide: Jesus' Master Class for Life* (Grand Rapids: Zondervan, 2010), 12.

Chapter Ten

THE "YOU DO YOU" GOSPEL

When it comes to regular, daily disciplines—the middle ground has always been a tough place for me to hang out. The extremes are where I feel most comfortable, and where I do my best work. In so many of my regular disciplines, I can feel the wind blowing through my hair as I swing from one side of the pendulum to the other.

I've either got to be ridiculously strict in my eating or eat whatever I want.

I'll choose to exercise rigorously or not at all.

When it comes to social media, I tend to shut it all down or place no limits on my time. Naturally, I'm either drowning in the demands of perfectionistic tendencies or floating down the lazy river without a care in the world.

After experiencing a taste of freedom from an acrobatic, work-based faith, I found the same degree of pendulum swinging in my Christian walk, too. I would swing from rigid Bible reading to disregarding it and living primarily off my feelings. I swung between ministries that encouraged guilt-driven obedience to those that dabbled in the prosperity gospel and self-guided spirituality. My view of God was either one of disappointment in my inability to do things right, or indifference to how I lived my life. I will admit, life on a pendulum brought an initial thrill. But after a while, I inevitably ended up dizzy, disoriented, and wanting to throw up.

As humans, I think our natural reaction in making choices is to overcorrect. If we don't find success in one area, we swing to the complete opposite side of the spectrum, hoping to find freedom and breakthrough there. If rigidity doesn't work, we swing to tolerance. When discipline exhausts us, we swing to disorder. We become obsessed with following the rules, or we disregard them completely.

If this is our natural, human tendency in worldly practices, you better believe that at some point, we will try to follow Jesus using a pendulum pattern. I believe Paul was very familiar with our human tendency to do this and therefore found it necessary to address it in his letter to the church at Galatia. (We've been learning a lot from Paul, amen?!) Paul spent most of his letter talking about not being under the Law, being justified through faith, and being subject to the law of grace and the Spirit. But in the back of his mind, I'm sure he was considering the "pendulum swingers" and professional over correctors who might swing to the flip side and conclude that true freedom must then come from no restraint, no discipline, and permission to let go of the rope and live.

In the fifth chapter of Galatians, Paul paints a picture of the two pendulum extremes that he knew the believers might fall prey to. On one side stood law-abiding, and on the other stood licentiousness (living without restraint). He addresses the law-abiders by telling them: "For freedom, Christ set us free (Gal. 5:1). He went on to remind the believers of their freedom in Christ, warning them to not become slaves to the Law by becoming circumcised. By doing this, they would be submitting again to the Law and alienating themselves from Christ and the gospel of grace (Gal. 5:1–4). But he also addresses those who might be tempted to swing to licentiousness by initially reminding them, "you were called to be free, brothers and sisters" (Gal. 5:13). He went on to encourage them to not use their freedom as a license to sin, serve their fleshly desires, or abuse the grace that they'd been given. Both sides receive the same reminder from Paul: they are both called to freedom. This leads us to one conclusion: **freedom is not found on either extreme of the pendulum.** We might be tempted to think that on one side of the pendulum lies life in the flesh and on the other lies life in the Spirit. But the truth is that both sides of the pendulum only require that we operate in our flesh, not the Spirit. The extremes ask us to do only what is most natural to us. We're either hypercontrolling, or we take our hands off completely. We're fueled by hyperaction or inaction. We thrive as rule-followers or rule-breakers.

We've spent a lot of time talking about false gospels that keep us stuck in visible patterns of striving for acceptance, rule following, and behavior modification. We discussed that these behaviors are rooted in fleshly desire for control. However, we can also have the temptation to hear the good news about grace and assume our job is to swing to the opposite side of the pendulum, thinking, *I'm finally free of all that.* We might conclude that striving only occurs on one side of the pendulum; but the truth is, it also exists on the other. Any time we are operating out of our flesh, it will inevitably lead us to strive because we are not living in the freedom for which we've been created. Both sides keep us slaves to our flesh. But here's where the difference lies: legalism makes you a pet, and licentiousness makes you a puppet. Legalism makes you a pet—keeping you on a hamster wheel, chasing this idea of fleshly perfection, acceptance, and being enough. **You are not free.** Licentiousness makes you a puppet—enslaving you to the passions, desires, and whims of your flesh to the point where you aren't controlling your choices; they are controlling you. **You are not free.** Both sides promise a freedom they cannot deliver. And the pursuit of this false promise will inevitably keep us stuck striving for it.

A False Kind of Freedom

Just as Paul warned the Galatian believers about not using their freedom as a license to sin, Peter also cautioned his readers against this same thing. In his second letter, Peter warns the believers about false teachers infiltrating their churches and preaching a false gospel of freedom. These false teachers went around promising that true freedom could be found by following one's fleshly desires, indulging in sexual pleasures, and essentially living without restraint. These teachers held the knowledge of the gospel yet found themselves tangled up in desire, preaching that living without restraint was how to be truly free. In other words, they preached that living with parameters is bondage and living without them is freedom. The banner staked in the middle of this false gospel says freedom is found in doing what you want, with this tagline right below: *You do you, boo*. If it feels good to your body, why deny it? This "You Do You" Gospel recruits disciples by promising them choice. In our culture, the declarations of this gospel might sound like:

> You wanna please yourself by overindulging in food? Go for it.
> Forget your struggles through intoxication? It's fine!
> Satisfy your jealousy by ripping apart another person through gossip? What's the harm?
> Escape your feelings of loneliness through pornographic movies, novels, or fantasies? You deserve it.
> Visiting mediums because you're freaked out about your future? Why not!

> Make decisions based on selfish ambition? Great, take care of yourself.
> Take out your anger on your spouse, family member, supposed friend, or coworker by trashing their character to others? You're just venting!
> Escape your own reality through hours of mindless scrolling and Netflix binging? It's just me-time!

The "You Do You" Gospel encourages you to feed your flesh what it desires, proclaiming that true freedom is found in the absence of restraint. But what it won't tell you is the painful side effect that happens when you indulge your flesh over and over and over: the placement of hooks. When we live our lives to the whims and desires of our flesh, it is almost like little hooks being placed into our skin. Decision by decision, hook by hook, one small habit turns into a routine, and more surface area becomes peppered with hooks. Like little strings tied to the ends of those hooks, temptation comes and fleshly desire pulls on those hooks. Every tug causes an itch-like sensation that needs to be scratched. And we scratch it. With every tug, we're moved by the demands of our flesh. You know what else has the appearance of a person but is attached and controlled by strings? A puppet. It is completely at the will and demands of whatever is pulling the strings. And that is what we become when we live our lives according to a gospel that tells us to just do what we want to do—whatever feels right, whatever feels good, whatever feels comfortable. We aren't free at all. That is why Peter says this about the false teachers preaching along the lines of this false gospel:

> They promise them freedom, but they themselves are slaves of corruption, since people are enslaved to whatever defeats them. (2 Pet. 2:19)

They were promising a freedom they didn't even have. Because the truth is whatever overcomes you, ultimately enslaves you. If we are overcome by our flesh, we are enslaved to its every want. Here's the truth: real freedom happens when the strings snap. When the hooks come out. When you aren't subject to bowing to your flesh and having to eat the consequences of guilt and shame. We are called to something greater: actual freedom. But this freedom doesn't happen by coming under the authority of ourselves; it comes through submitting ourselves under the authority of Someone else.

Freedom by the Spirit

The problem with the "You Do You" Gospel is that it ignores the reality that when we put our trust in Jesus, we received an entirely new nature and a new Lord. Where we once only had the capacity to sin and serve ourselves, we now have the capacity for godliness because the Spirit of the living God now lives inside us. The Spirit makes all the difference. Where our flesh made us puppets and strivers, the Spirit sets us free as sons and daughters because "where the Spirit of the Lord is, there is freedom" (2 Cor. 3:17). It is only under his authority that we experience freedom.

Real freedom.

Because we've received new identities, new desires, new dreams, new vision, new hope, and the reality of a new home, true freedom is found when we walk in those identities as God's children; not gratifying our old nature that leads to death but by walking in the Spirit who leads to life (John 6:63).

True freedom is living loved—yes, really loved—convinced that his love is yours in Christ. It is walking in all that he declares over you and letting go of what others have spoken over you. It is trusting him a thousand times over, believing he is altogether good and does good. True freedom is found in dying to self and what is important to **me** and coming alive in Christ and loving what is important to **him**. Freedom is bowing at the feet of Jesus, thanking him for his approval over us rather than chasing after the approval of everyone else. Freedom is found in giving him our every "yes" because we will find him faithful every time.

Freedom is inseparable from our new nature, and it is absolutely impossible to attain while living according to our old one. Christ promises us a freedom our flesh can never deliver. The gospel of grace has called us away from living according to our flesh and out of a life of striving. If freedom is found not in law abiding or law avoiding, where then do we go?

Freed From—Freed To

We are called to come down from the extremes of the left and right and come to holy ground. You must know that this middle place is where we live by the Spirit. However, this is where we will actively feel the opposition and tension of our flesh most intensely. Crazily enough, on an actual pendulum, when the string of the pendulum is in the middle (also known as the "mean position") this is where the contraption is holding the most tension. The highest point of tension isn't found in extremes, but in the middle. You and I? We are invited to live smack dab in the middle of the pendulum, in the place where we will feel the most tension because this is the place where we cannot live naturally. The problem with living in the extremes is that they require no reliance on the Spirit. But here, in the dead middle, is where we must live our lives—in the middle of the tension, when we want to run to an extreme that brings comfort instead of relying on the Spirit, in whom we can really trust. And truthfully? Walking by the Spirit will feel tense because our flesh and our Spirit are at war (Gal. 5:17). But here in the middle—in the laying down of our lives, in the reliance on the Spirit, in the denial of our flesh, in the seeking of his kingdom, and in embracing our new identities as children of God—we find freedom. Freedom that makes you want to run wild.

You and I—we are free.
We have been freed.
From the power and penalty of sin.
From the control of our flesh.
From a life of living for ourselves.
From guilt and shame.
From trying hard to earn God's love and keep it.
From a life of wondering if God truly loves us.
From a mind that is set on pleasing other people.
From hamster wheels and puppet strings.
From a life of striving and trying to be enough for God.

I could go on and on about what the gospel has freed us from, but from here on out, let's talk about all the life-giving, earth-shaking, soul-liberating things the gospel has freed us to.

REFLECT & RESPOND

1. The "You Do You" Gospel centers around limiting perceived restraint. What kind of things in culture do you see believers encouraged to participate in that fall in line with this false gospel?

2. Is there any area of your life where you aren't experiencing freedom and feel like your choices are controlling you? If so, what areas?

PART THREE

WHAT THE GOSPEL FREES US TO

The beauty of what Jesus has done is that we've not only been freed from something, but he's also freed us to something even better. Grace is a whole new way to live. We are free to receive love deeply in a way we may never have experienced. We are free to enjoy God because of who he is. We are free to set others free with this good news that broke off our shackles and delivered our hearts. We are free to run wild as children of God who have grown increasingly confident in his unwavering love for us on our best and worst days. A strained relationship caused by striving for approval has now transformed into a trust-filled relationship that is free to grow into all it was designed to be. Let's discover the beauty in all the glorious things we've been freed to. At the end of each chapter, you'll find the "Experiencing Freedom Guide"—a tool to help you process these truths and put these realities into practice.

Chapter Eleven

FREE TO LOVE AND BE LOVED

If I could give advice to someone wanting real, authentic community in their lives, I would tell them this: find you some friends who won't be afraid to hurt your feelings for the sake of your freedom. Friends who aren't about your happiness but your healthiness and holiness. Friends who fight for your freedom are gifts from God.

A year ago, I had three of my freedom-fighting friends approach me in the same week about an unhealthy relationship pattern they saw in my life—and they all said almost the same thing.

- "We're seeing you back off and ignore the people you're investing in because it's grown uncomfortable and challenging."
- "You're taking your hands off of relationships because they're hard."
- "You went radio silent in our friendship when I needed you to speak up the most."

I couldn't defend myself because every word they said was true. During this season, several of my friends were struggling with their faith or going through hard times in general. In this incredibly difficult time, instead of walking through hard things with them, being honest, and still pursuing them in the midst of it, I backed off. I took my hands off and backed up until they could get their lives together, or until everything could be normal and we could be close again.

Those three encounters with my friends caused me to question why backing off and shrinking back was my default setting in relationships, especially when they got tough. Through the help of the Holy Spirit and trusted friendships, I came to realize four things:

1. I will ultimately love others the way I think I am loved.
2. To the capacity that I believe I am loved is the degree I will love others.
3. The conditions under which I'm loved will be directly reflected in the kind of love I give away.
4. What I truly believe about love will be most evident in the way I love other people—especially when things are hard.

In this particular season and really in so many others, the way I was loving other people spoke volumes about how I believed God loved me. The harsh truth I faced was that the way I loved people was undeniably broken because what I believed about God's love was broken. And this is true of us today: our ability to love others will be a direct reflection of the ways we believe God loves us. We will give love the same way we think we receive it.

Seeing God through Shame and Fear

We know God is love. We know this—we sing about this—we preach about this. But the way we love others will be the litmus test as to how we believe we are really loved and on what terms we are loved. After all, Jesus said people will know we are his disciples by how we love others (John 13:35). The proof is in the pudding. While there are numerous ways we can view God's love, I believe there are two primary lenses through which we can view God's love that keep us stuck in striving: shame and fear.

The False Narrative of Shame: God Loves Me Conditionally

A conditional love is one that is given according to correct behaviors—requirements being met—and is only granted under certain terms. If we believe God loves us conditionally, then we will attempt to meet these conditions created by our own expectations and perceptions. But, of course, we will not be able to meet them all. As a result, we will experience shame. Shame is the humiliation we feel when we think we've done something wrong, improper, or disgraceful. In our shame-ridden state, we will try to hide from God, deny our guilt by trying to outweigh the good with the bad, or attempt to undo our wrongdoing by trying hard to come back with better. When we view God through our shame, our motives are to appease him. We inherently believe that God pours out his love in our good behavior and withholds love from us in our bad behavior.

Naturally, if we believe God loves us conditionally, we will choose to love others only under certain conditions. We will come close when they are making the right decisions, when they meet our expectations, when we agree, and when things aren't hard. In the same token, we might find ourselves backing up when we don't agree, when decisions are made that we don't approve of, or during another kind of struggle. The sad part is that when we love others this way, we are communicating to them that they must earn our love and work to keep it. Not to mention, this causes the other person in the relationship to feel like our love can be taken away from them at any given moment.

The False Narrative of Fear: God Loves Me Competitively

A competitive love is one that operates under limits. There is a scarce supply of love, and it is given to those who are doing the best job. If God loves competitively, then his bucket of love is dished out to the ones who are loving him, serving him, and honoring him in the greatest measure. Our response to this kind of love is fear—not a holy, reverent fear that leads to wisdom (Prov. 1:7) but fear that we are going to be punished (1 John 4:18). If we aren't the best performer, our perceived punishment is that we don't get love. Our fear fuels us to work harder than anybody else so that we will be loved by God. Therefore, our motivation for serving God and obeying him is sheerly fear based because we don't want to miss out on being loved.

This narrative leaves us believing that **we've got to compete for love**. As a relational result, it turns other Christ-followers into competition. We don't see other followers of Christ as coheirs but as competitors. If we believe we are loved competitively, we will feel threatened by other people's walks with the Lord. We will find ourselves jealous when we hear of others having longer Bible study time, more consistent prayer, hearing clearly from the Lord, or seeing how he is working in their lives in miraculous ways. Instead of celebrating them in that moment, we will feel the need to be better than they are so they don't get the love that could be ours. When we love this way, we won't experience the joy, warmth, strength, and comfort that comes from community, but rather the bitterness, strife, envy, and jealousy that splinters friendships faster than anything else. We can't celebrate people and hold contempt for them at the same time.

Thanks be to the God of heaven who does not love conditionally, nor does he love competitively. His love is better than we could ever hope.

Letting His Love Wash over Us

In the introduction of this book, I talked about a monumental moment with the Lord during worship when he addressed my resistance and called out my rebellion against his love. I was flailing my arms and singing about the love of God washing over me when in fact I was actually refusing to let it wash over me. It didn't feel right. It went against every single cell in my human nature to let the God of love just . . . love me—with no strings attached. In my pride, I wanted to prove I was worthy of love—that God made a good choice when he saved me. Receiving love is an act of humility, and, gosh, we have to let him love us.

I often think of the story of Peter in his obstinance and stubbornness, refusing to let Jesus wash his feet. I identify with him all too well. Shortly before Jesus was betrayed, he pulled all his disciples together to celebrate the Passover Festival, and here he would demonstrate his love for them in a very unexpected way. Scripture prefaces this event by saying this of Jesus: "Having loved his own who were in the world, he loved them to the end" (John 13:1 NIV). After dinner, Jesus got up, took off his outer clothing, wrapped a cloth around his waist, and started washing the disciples' feet. But when it came time for Jesus to wash Peter's feet, Peter resisted and refused. Peter declared: "No! You shall never wash my feet!"

I can't blame him. If anything, Peter should be washing Jesus's feet, right? This job of washing feet was grimy. (This is exactly why I did *not* jump on the "wash your new husband's feet at your wedding ceremony" bandwagon!) This task was reserved for the lowliest servant to perform. And here was the Son of God, on his knees, offering to wash the most dirt-ridden part of Peter's body.

But Jesus responded to Peter's refusal with a severe statement: "Unless I wash you, you have no part with me" (John 13:8 NIV). No part with me—talk about an ultimatum! Eventually, Peter did allow Jesus to wash his feet, but it took Jesus's rebuking and calling out Peter's pride to do it. Jesus's humbling act modeled the way of self-sacrifice and love—this is the essence of the Father. The disciples would be the first tangible recipients of this sacrificial love, and when Jesus was finished, he told them they should go and do what he did for them. He sent them to go and show the same kind of sacrificial, humility-driven love they had just been recipients of. I know God is not formulaic, but I will say I do enjoy when he gives us an equation and order for how things work! **We receive his love *then* repeat love**.

Had Peter clung to his pride, refusing to receive this sacrificial love, how in the world could he emulate it to the world? The same is true for us. We can't be messengers of love unless we follow the order Jesus modeled: receive then repeat. We've been running for such a long time, trying to prove our worth, earn our keep, and strive for a place at his table. It's time to retire those worn-out shoes of striving and let him wash over us with his love. Because this isn't a love you have to run for to receive. In fact, it's a love that ran all the way to hell and back to rescue you. A love that chose to lay his life down before you could ever do anything good, right, or praiseworthy. It is not love you have to compete for. His love is that which is freely given and stands ready to wash all over you. It is given without measure, and it is never going to run dry. It will not skip over you. It's a love that, once received, will send you running to give it away in the same way it came to you.

But this is a love we can push away for a whole lot of lesser loves. And in our running, we're living loveless—striving for it in all the wrong places.

Friend, will you let love in?

Holy Spirit, will you help us let love in?

Resting in His Love

You know what I think our hearts are really longing for? A love that is secure. We want a love that can't be taken away from us. A love that will always have eyes for us. Love that won't back up when life gets hard, panic when we're bleeding out, or wrinkle its nose when we've messed up—again. Our heart is desperate for a love that takes our hand, pulls us close, looks us straight in the eyes, and says: "I'm *never* going to let you go—and I've never made a promise I didn't keep." We want a love that doesn't fluctuate, that we can bank on every single day. And I'm here to tell you, there is such good news for your heart today.

That love is yours. Today, tomorrow, and always. We crave this kind of love because we were crafted for this kind of love. We were made in the image of a creator who created the caverns of our heart to be satisfied—truly and completely—by his love alone. And our hearts won't stop running until we rest in him and in his love. St. Augustine says it perfectly in his book *Confessions*: "You have made us for yourself, and our hearts are restless until they rest in you."[1] There is rest for the runner today, there is rest for you. You can take a deep breath because here is what's true:

- In his love, God became the remedy, through Jesus, to rescue us from the power of sin that separated us from him.
- Because of Jesus's sacrifice, our sins will not be held against us—there is now no condemnation for those of us in Christ.
- God sees us through the perfection of his Son—we are brought into his family as children, fiercely loved by love himself. He is the Father of all fathers. He does it best.

- God gave us his Spirit to lead us, teach us, correct us, and guide us—he knows we can't do this on our own.
- You will stumble. You will fail. You will be super immature sometimes. But his love won't back up. It will lean in. It will meet you in your mess, call you higher, and give you the power to rise. True love disciplines.
- When we sin, we can approach the throne of Grace, and he is faithful to forgive us. He won't shame us when we come. His kindness leads our hearts to true repentance. As we trust what God has spoken over us and believe who he says we are, our hearts actually begin to genuinely want him more than we want sin.
- God's love is covenantal, not conditional. He has promised us himself, and he will never break that promise.
- We don't run *for* love; we are empowered *by* love. God's love will compel us and propel us into the good works God has planned for us to walk into. This love is the best news in the world—his heart longs for people to experience and believe his love.
- We can trust his love, and we can trust his heart. As we mature, we will believe him more and more—growing quicker in saying yes to the things he calls us to because we're convinced of his goodness.

We can rest in this love. We can trust that we are secure in it now, and we will continue to be secure as we mature and learn to trust him even more. He's in it for the long haul. His love is here to stay.

Reflecting His Love

The crazy part of all this is that the more we receive and learn from his love, the more it will ooze out of us. The love of God is like no other; it is catalytic. We always talk about how hurt people, hurt people. But guess what? The opposite is true: loved people, *love people*! This is the way God intended it. We love because he first loved us (1 John 4:19). Not only this, but we will love in the same fashion he loves us—sacrificially, unconditionally, and noncompetitively.

When we try to love others out of duty, obligation, or as a result of our striving, it is a cheap imitation of the real thing. It doesn't point to the God of love because it isn't real love. It's the toxic fruit of our proving and striving—it's pride. We must first receive the love of God so we can reflect that same love to the people around us.

Friend, as you sit under the ever-pouring fountain of his love, let it run over you in every place. And watch as it pours out of you into every space of your life.

In the way you invest in your family.
In how you selflessly love in your marriage.
In the way you place courage and security into your kids.
In how you invest and commit in your friendships.
In the way you build up the body of Christ.
In how you reach out to the hurting, the broken, the needy.
In the ways you love God back.

Oh, one of the most beautiful things we are free to do is love him back. Because our feet are now running to him to enjoy him and love on him instead of running around doing things for him to earn his love. Let us never lose sight of this truth: it all starts with him. It is all because of him. The author, giver, and creator of love itself. Dear friend, won't you let him love you today? I promise, it will radically transform the way you love others. You are free to love and be loved.

EXPERIENCING FREEDOM GUIDE

Reflect

It's amazing how the way we love others will be reflective of how we believe God loves us. When we receive the love of God, we are then able to repeat and emulate that same kind of love to the people around us. When we do, we'll notice that loving others comes from the place of overflow in our lives instead of something we are trying to muster up or even fake.

Journal

1. Just like Peter, we can refuse the gift the Lord is offering us, namely, his love. What are some of the things that hinder you from receiving God's love? Is it your guilt? Shame? Fear? Or even pride that you don't need to receive love? Take a few minutes and jot those things down.

_____

_____

_____

_____

_____

_____

_____

_____

2. We talked about two misperceived ways we can view God's love: through fear or shame. Which one, if either, do you find yourself relating with? How has that affected your relationships with God and others?

_____

_____

_____

_____

_____

_____

Write It & Memorize It

"Love consists in this: not that we loved God, but that he loved us and sent his Son to be the atoning sacrifice for our sins. Dear friends, if God loved us in this way, we also must love one another. No one has ever seen God. If we love one another, God remains in us and his love is made complete in us." —1 John 4:10–12

Call to Action

On a sticky note, write the prayer: "Lord, show me how to receive your love today," and place it on your bedside table. Each morning this week, whisper that prayer as you set your feet on the floor, and consciously be on the lookout for ways that God demonstrates his love for you each day.

Note

[1] Augustine of Hippo, *Confessions*, Book 1 of 8, ed. and trans. Carolyn J. B. Hammond (Cambridge, MA: Harvard University Press, 2016), 3.

Chapter Twelve

FREE TO TRUST

One of my most treasured birthday presents came when I turned twenty years old: layers and layers and *more layers* of snow. College classes were cancelled, blankets of ice covered our cars, and the entire town of Portales was buying food and supplies to last for a few days inside. As a longtime desert rat, I can count on my hands the number of times I've been snowed in. This felt like the kindest birthday present ever.

As I sat at my kitchen table admiring the snow and reflecting on my twenty years of life, I started thinking about all my favorite childhood memories, sentimental moments, and times I loved as a kid. In the middle of my quest down memory lane, I remembered the book *You Are Special* by Max Lucado. I adored this book as a kid. My parents read it to me all the time, and we physically exhausted the VHS movie version. I thought, *I should watch that again for memory's sake!*

What was supposed to be a sweet, reminiscent viewing turned into a hysterical sobbing session at my kitchen table. I was beside myself—laughing and crying uncontrollably at the same time. It must have been comical to watch. I had never listened to this book as an adult, and it spoke to me in a much deeper way. The message in this little children's book hit me like a ton of bricks that day and gave me words to ask God for a freedom I wasn't living in. If you've never read this book, first of all, you need to read it! But until then, I'll give you a little synopsis. The story is about a town of wooden creatures called Wemmicks who live based on a star and dot system. When they achieve great things, other people give them stars. When they mess up, they receive grey dots. One day, a worn-out, dot-covered Wemmick named Punchinello met a woman named Lucia who had no stars or dots. Upon his asking, Lucia revealed her stickerless secret: every day, she went and met their maker—Eli—and he reminded her about who she was and whom he created her to be. Because of his word over her and her trust in what he said, nobody's stars or dots meant anything to her, so they didn't stick. She trusted him above everything else—above *everyone* else.

This little wooden chick, fictitious as she may be, was free. And I was so desperate for that kind of freedom. On my twentieth birthday, I walked away from my kitchen table with a choice between two ways to live: a lifestyle of trying to **please God** and others by becoming the best version of me, or a lifestyle of **trusting God,** abiding in who he is and what he had already spoken over me.

Needless to say, I still chose the first lifestyle for many years, and it was draining. But along the way God, in his grace, grabbed my hand and helped me walk differently. Now, I have experienced the second, and I have to say: this must be the abundant life Jesus was talking about. This is freedom—and I don't ever want to get over it.

A Heart That Trusts First

You might be thinking, "Wait, wait, wait. Shouldn't we want to please God? Isn't that the goal?" To that I would say, yes. Pleasing God is the goal. But what I'm calling into question here is how we go about it. It all boils down to the fuel: Is trusting God through faith the fuel for pleasing God? Or is performance in the flesh the fuel? Because in the end, one will actually please God and the other will not. Scripture is clear: "Those who are in the flesh cannot please God" (Rom. 8:8 ESV).

When our sole purpose is to please God first, we inevitably begin manufacturing all kinds of "good things" to make or keep God happy with us without actually putting our trust in him. However, we are given the remedy in Hebrews 11:6: "without faith it is impossible to please [God]" (ESV). Faith and trust in Jesus are the root of our godliness—they are the foundation. As a result, pleasing God is the fruit of our trust in him.

Trueface Ministries has been so instrumental in my understanding of this concept. In one of their teachings, they explain this idea of faith and trust:

> The word "faith" is the noun form of the word "believe" or "trust." Thus, the issue of pleasing God is inextricably bound to trusting Him. What the author of Hebrews is saying is that **pleasing God is the result of trusting Him**. There is nothing that we can "conjure up" to please Him that is not based upon who He is and what He has already done in and for us.[1]

A heart that trusts is convinced and confident in the sufficiency of the death and resurrection of Jesus to pay for sins, a brand-new nature and identity, the Holy Spirit's empowerment, and God's faithfulness to mature them and lead them from here until eternity. The woman who trusts in who God is and what Jesus has done is free to run into the good things he's prepared because she shares in his oneness—she is about what *he* is about. Her eyes are locked on his because she is assured of his love. She isn't running from him; she's running *with* him. Christ is in her.

When our primary motivation is trusting what God says about himself, others, and even ourselves, we begin to walk differently. It sounds like some kind of magic, but as we walk in trust, we begin to become whom we were created to be. We mature into the very things God has spoken over us—they are true of us because he said them. Walking in a broken identity that isn't rooted in trusting God will leave us stuck as acrobats trying to prove that the worst things about us aren't true. But when our hearts seek to trust God first, above all else, we are fueled and filled by the love of God, confident that we are saved by his grace. At our core, we believe our sins are not held against us, we are adopted as children, given a brand-new nature, and sealed with the very Spirit of God. As followers of Jesus, our lives are no longer about achievement and what we can do for God, but rather about coming into agreement with what God deems important, what he says about himself, and what he says about us. Walking in agreement with God is one of the most powerful things we can do.

Agreement over Achievement

I walked through a tough season last year where I felt overwhelmed with lies about my identity, my own inadequacies, and my shortcomings. These lies produced an insatiable hunger to prove that the worst things about me weren't true. With some help, I discovered I had made many agreements with these lies, one of them being that if I could not do something perfectly, it meant I was incompetent and incapable of doing it, period. When we make agreements with lies, it's almost as if we shake hands with them to seal the deal and say, "Okay! I will live by that." Therefore, in the face of all these inadequacies I was feeling, I met them with trying to *prove* my competence and ability. One of the more silly, superficial inadequacies I'd been fighting with (along with the way more serious others) was feeling abnormally anxious when driving in big cities with people in my car. Listen, I'm a straight grandma driver at heart. I love the slow and steady pace I get to drive in my small town, getting to soak in that good song playing in the car. But put me in unfamiliar territory at an intersection with six turning lanes or on busy highways, and suddenly, I turn into Letty from *Fast and Furious*. I pretend like there are no rules and all signs are suggestions. I get a little cray cray. This is not because I am wildly confident but because I'm actually very nervous and uncomfortable.

Every time I drove in a larger city with someone in my car, I'd remind myself of that little agreement I made: I show myself and other people I am competent by making no mistakes. (And in this case, no mistakes in driving.)

My husband, Lance, has always been a great advocate of coming into agreement with what God says about us. I'll tell you what, this man isn't afraid to call out an identity lie and coerce you to yell at that lie out loud, break your agreement with it, and say *that is not true about me* until you believe it. And he made me confront that untrue agreement when my inner Letty took the wheel, driving in a big city one weekend. Let's just say a last-minute, fast-and-furious type of right turn in a straight only lane completely wrecked my "no mistakes mantra" and left my husband with his jaw wide open, gripping the side of the passenger seat. In that moment, I experienced the repercussions of the agreement and concluded it must be true: I must actually be totally incompetent.

The tears came in hot on the way home as I not only felt the embarrassment of my reckless driving incident, but really as I contemplated the truth of all the other very real, more serious inadequacies I was feeling and lies I was believing about them. As they flooded through my mind, I blurted out loud to my husband: "What if **it's all** true? What if I am *all* the things I fear I am? What if the worst things about me are true?" Line by line, I began listing all the lies I was viciously wrestling with when it came to my identity:

- My body is broken.
- My mind is broken.
- God chose the absolute wrong person to do the things he's asked.
- I am fundamentally incompetent.
- I am no help to anyone.
- I have nothing to contribute to the people in my life.
- I'm an awful friend.
- I'll always be controlled by what people think.
- I will always be a coward.

As soon as I finished listing off all those thoughts, my husband Lance put our car in park at the light at an intersection and said, "I am not moving this car until you say those things aren't true—say it!"

To which I stubbornly stated, "No."

"Kaitlin! Say it right now—'Those things are not true of me.'"

"NO! You're gonna be stuck here *all* day and get a ticket waiting for me to say it."

"Well, I'm not moving this car out of park until you do."

Stubborn man. I mumbled the dang words, and we kept driving. But I love what he said moments after: "I'll bet that if you quit agreeing with all these untrue things, you'll actually begin to believe what *is* true about you." And he was right. We make these kinds of agreements all the time with ourselves:

- I can never say no to people—I'm such a pushover.
- I won't ever be able to understand all this because I'm not smart.
- To be a strong woman, I have to be perfect in every area of my life.
- If I'm wrong about something, I'm not hearing God at all.
- This relationship will never be reconciled—it's too hard and we've gone through too much.
- My body always betrays me—it doesn't look the way I want or do what it should.

We also make them about God:

- I've got to work hard for God to love me and see my worth.
- I am one mistake away from God abandoning me.
- God is most pleased with me when I am serving in ministry.
- Intimacy with God is directly tied to my effort.
- I become who God wants me to be by trying hard.
- God punishes me through his silence.
- When I sin, I need to come back with better behavior to prove to God I'm really changing.

The problem with these agreements is that they are not in alignment with what God has deemed to be true about himself or us. If we walk according to these agreements, we will spend our lives trying to prove that those things aren't true. It's a ruthless distraction that keeps us self-destructing, self-improving, and more than anything, self-focused.

But I believe God has given us a better way—to not spend our lives walking in our flesh trying to prove but to make practice of living in agreement with God. Instead of denying weakness, we own it and press on according to his strength. We bring our fear, inadequacies, and hesitation before the throne of God and take the next step according to his power. We confess our unbelief, confusion, and lack of direction and then walk according to his wisdom. Life is so much better when we live it according to his strength, his power within us, his righteousness, his divine design, his wisdom, his timing, and his final word. When we do this, we put our trust in his unending well of resources and strength instead of spending decades trying to dig up wells that will always run dry.

Let's Get in Alignment and Agreement

I have a wall in my closet that is plastered with verses that remind me to agree with what God has spoken about my standing with him, the sufficient work of Jesus, the Spirit's role in my life, the process of maturing, the freedom I have in Christ, and the words he has spoken about my identity. These passages remind me that I am free to trust him, to take him at his word, to bank on his promises, and to declare these things as truth even when I don't want to believe them. If you would like to, feel free to write these agreements down on index cards, look up the Scripture references, write them below the statements, put them in a place you can see and say them every day. This is a powerful practice that reminds us of what is true, helping us to walk in trust and agreement instead of striving.

Please know these verses aren't some self-help, word of faith, prosperity affirmations where you repeat stuff to make yourself feel better or to somehow just speak the things you want into existence. No, this is taking God's Word and his promises and saying back to him, "God, I choose today to agree with you on this. I'm going to walk in this today because I absolutely trust you."

DAILY AGREEMENTS

I've been given a new heart with new passion, steadfastness, and desires. (Ezek. 36:26)

I am infused with and empowered by the Spirit of God. (Eph. 1:13; Col. 1:27–29)

I've been made right with God—it is done. (Gal. 2:16; 1 Cor. 6:11)

I am God's dearly loved child. (Gal. 3:26, 4:7)

Nothing can separate me from God's love. (Rom. 8:31–39)

I can come boldly before God. (Heb. 4:16)

I am being made new, day by day. (2 Cor. 5:17)

My eternity is secure, and my salvation doesn't fluctuate. (John 6:37; John 5:24)

I can trust God's love even in the midst of "maturing" behaviors. (Rom. 5:1; Col. 3:9–10)

Sin is not in charge of me anymore. (Rom. 6:6, 14)

The way I love others is a reflection of God's love. (John 13:34–35)

God's mercies are new each morning. (Lam. 3:22–23)

God's faithfulness in the past proves I can trust his timing in the future. (Prov. 3:5–6)

I represent Christ to other people! (2 Cor. 5:20)

I have a sound mind, not a spirit of fear. (2 Tim. 1:7)

The more familiar we get with what God says about us and about himself, the less time we will spend struggling through a tangled web of lies and the more time we will enjoy walking in trust, living in the freedom of who he's created us to be.

EXPERIENCING FREEDOM GUIDE

Reflect

Pleasing God is a good motive, but our primary motivation should be trusting God. Our ultimate trust pleases God; it is the fruit! What would it look like to trust the promises God has declared in Scripture, both about himself and us? What would it look like to take all those words into account and answer back, "I trust your words are true and will walk in them—I believe you, God"?

Journal

1. What are some of the ways that you've tried to go about pleasing God? What habits have you formed, believing that those are the things that make God pleased with you?

_____

_____

_____

_____

_____

2. In this chapter, we talked about agreements we make with ourselves that contradict what God says about us. Take a few minutes and jot down every "agreement" you can think of that you have made about yourself or others.

_____

Write It & Memorize It

"Trust in him at all times, you people; pour out your hearts to him, for God is our refuge." —Psalm 62:8 (NIV)

"You will keep in perfect peace those whose minds are steadfast, because they trust in you. Trust in the LORD forever, for the LORD, the LORD himself, is the Rock eternal." —Isaiah 26:3–4 (NIV)

Call to Action

Take a look at all the agreements you wrote down in the journaling prompt section. This week, research Scriptures that counteract those false agreements with the truth of what God says about you. Write those Scriptures where you can see them, make them your lock screen on your phone, and commit them to memory. Then, when you are tempted to believe one of those old false agreements, you can whip out the Word of God and instead declare: God I trust and agree with what *you* have to say about this instead of what I'm tempted to believe.

Note

[1] "Exhausted: Why Pleasing God Can't Be Our First Motivation," Trueface, February 25, 2020, https://www.trueface.org/blog/2020/2/19/exhausted-why-pleasing-god-cant-be-our-first-motivation.

Chapter Thirteen

FREE TO NEED

"God, no offense—but when you made me, I feel like you set me up for failure." With all the honesty I could gather, I spat out those words in prayer to the Lord on my Tuesday morning commute to work. That particular week, I felt betrayed by my personality, frustrated with my energy limit, and overall annoyed with how I naturally stunk at a ton of things God calls believers to in Scripture.

- Being bold in faith
- Speaking honestly
- Readily telling my story in and out of season
- Sharing the gospel
- Remaining steadfast under trial
- Speaking up against injustice
- Speaking truth to my neighbor

As I pondered all these qualities that I saw in the life of Jesus and his followers, I mentally began rating myself in these areas and measuring my ability to do them. Well, that didn't take long because the answer to each was clear: **not very well**. Naturally, this led me to address all the areas in which I felt like I failed to measure up:

- I struggle to hold my ground in disagreement.
- I'm in love with what people think about me.
- I have a hard time being honest with people.
- I have a complicated relationship with sharing the gospel.
- I stumble *all* over my words when I'm explaining something.
- I would rather speak flattery that earns approval than truth that sets people free.
- I feel incapable of speaking up when I need to.
- Faking being fine is easier than addressing how I really feel.

As I made list after list accusing God of fashioning me with all the wrong characteristics, his gentle words interrupted my thoughts: *I didn't set you up for failure when I made you—I designed you to* **need** *me.*

Those words felt so backward and upside down for me because I'd been drifting in the currents of our independent, do-it-yourself culture for such a long time. I'd been groomed to daily assess my skill sets, measure them up against what was asked of me, and make a way for myself to just **do it**. I operated by eliminating my needs, playing off my strengths, and performing extra hard to cover my own inadequacy.

But the thought of being designed to need God brought my mind back to what God spoke to Paul: "My grace is sufficient for you, for my power is made perfect in weakness." And to this, Paul concluded: "Therefore I will boast all the more gladly of my weaknesses, so that the power of Christ may rest upon me" (2 Cor. 12:9 ESV).

At first, this call into a life of embracing weakness and need felt absolutely cringy. But as I thought about it more, I could feel the pressure leave my shoulders. The thought of owning—and boasting in—my weakness instead of covering it up felt like relief. The thought of not having to be perfect at everything allowed me to breathe. The thought of turning heavenward instead of inward in my inadequacy dismissed the pressure to perform. The thought of drawing from infinite resources instead of my frailty-ridden supply closet felt a whole lot like freedom. All these things? They are freedom. This life of leaning on Christ—this is the life the gospel liberates us to.

The Abundant, Dependent Life

I once heard it said that no one has ever been freer than Jesus. All throughout the Gospels, we see this reality to be true. Jesus lived his life by remaining ungripped by strongholds, letting the opinions of others go, and ridding himself of self-obsession to the point of laying down his life for others. Jesus is our model of total freedom. He brought to us the good news of the gospel, which leads us into this same type of freedom. Yet it wasn't his uncanny sense of independence, strength, or self-will that kept him free. In fact, it was quite the opposite. In the Gospels, we see Jesus saying as much:

> Very truly I tell you, the Son can do nothing by himself; he can do only what he sees his Father doing, because whatever the Father does the Son also does. (John 5:19 NIV)

> I do nothing on my own but speak just what the Father has taught me. (John 8:28 NIV)

In Jesus's words, we don't see the pursuit of independence—we see a divine tethering. If Jesus, the Son of God, fulfilled his earthly ministry not through his own independence but through utter dependence on the Father, why in the world would we be the exception?

The bottom line is that Jesus lived tethered to the Father. And this tethering didn't lead to a life of confinement but a life of liberty. It's hilarious to me how backward this is. Typically, when we think of being restrained or tethered by something, we imagine a prison or a confinement situation in which we don't have access to the best parts of our lives. Yet when we live disconnected from the Father's resources and do not rely on his Spirit, we are literally confined to a life of self-sufficiency. We marry ourselves to this leaky bucket filled with our own skills, wisdom, life experiences, and strength. We live our lives drawing from the same well, with the same dirty water, with the same limitations, and the same inevitable outcome: the water will run out and we will burn out. **Self-sufficiency is a spiritual form of house arrest that keeps us stuck, sheltered, and shackled to a life of scarcity.**

This is not the abundant life Jesus calls us to! As Jesus says in John 10:10: "I have come so that they may have life and have it in abundance." Oddly enough, when we look at the context both before and after this verse, we find that this abundance Jesus talks about is a byproduct of embracing our design to need him. In the surrounding verses, Jesus compares his relationship with his followers to sheep and a shepherd. We are the sheep and he is our guide who leads us every step of the way. This relationship Jesus compares himself and his followers to is a completely dependent one—and that should tell us something. The abundant life is a dependent one, and a self-sufficient life is a scarce one.

Two Kinds of Trust

As a visual learner, I truly appreciate the contrasting picture of abundance versus scarcity that God paints for us through the words of the prophet Jeremiah. If I could give this word picture a title, I would call it "A Tale of Two Trees." Let's lean into the picture and examine the strokes. In Jeremiah 17, the prophet writes:

> Cursed is the person who trusts in mankind.
> He makes human flesh his strength,
> and his heart turns from the LORD. (v. 5)

Just like we talked about in Chapter One, when we place our trust and assurance in our own righteousness, strength, resources, and goodness, we resist the need for God and our hearts slowly turn inward and away from the Lord. Assurance in ourselves completely eliminates the need for God and his Spirit. Dependence on our own flesh is a characteristic of our life before Christ and it cannot produce godliness (Rom. 8:8).

> He will be like a juniper in the Arabah;
> he cannot see when good comes
> but dwells in the parched places in the wilderness,
> in a salt land where no one lives. (Jer. 17:6)

The one who dwells in self-reliance is much like this desert shrub, rooted in a land of scarcity. It is confined to a limited supply of nutrients, stunted in growth because of its lack of nutrients, and completely alone without a community. This plant's environment keeps it from being dependent on anything other than itself. It cannot bear fruit or become the tree it was designed to be because salt lands don't allow for healthy growth. Striving ultimately leads us to these parched places because we've convinced ourselves that we don't need to rely on anything but ourselves, just like the desert plant. And as a result, this tree cannot produce fruit or provide shade.

> The person who trusts in the Lord,
> whose confidence indeed is the Lord, is blessed.
> He will be like a tree planted by water:
> it sends its roots out toward a stream,
> it doesn't fear when heat comes,
> and its foliage remains green.
> It will not worry in a year of drought
> or cease producing fruit. (Jer. 17:7–8)

This tale of two trees ultimately tells us about two ways to trust. The one who trusts in self dwells in the land of scarcity. But the one who trusts in the Lord, whose confidence is in him, dwells in a land of spiritual abundance. Notice that this second tree lives in a frequent state of need and dependence. It is not planted in isolated, parched places; it is planted in proximity to a power source. The root system of this tree seeks out the stream and soaks up its richness. The stream is the lifeblood of the tree—it causes goodness to emerge from its branches, protects it from shriveling up when it's hot, and keeps it steady when everything around it is drying up. This tree is free to bear fruit, bring nourishment to others, provide shade, and give off healthy life-giving nutrients to the world around it. This is all because it is completely dependent on a life-giving stream. The tree grows and bears fruit not because of its own effort and self-will but because of what it is abiding in.

As Christ-followers, we are called to live like the second tree. We are one with Christ and are called to abide in him. Part of our personal death and resurrection means we leave behind a life of self-sufficiency and instead choose to walk daily in a posture of

Holy Spirit-sufficiency. The Holy Spirit is our help, our empowerment, our wisdom, and our lifeline. We can trust him and bank on him all day, every day!

When we come up against inadequacy in our jobs, education, marriages, parenting, ministry, and general life issues, we often fall into patterns of thinking: "This is all up to me. I've got to be enough in this situation." And this simply isn't true. Left to our own "leaky bucket," we will find ourselves digging through a scarce number of resources. It will not be enough.

However, as believers, we have daily access to the Spirit who is in us, and we can come needy. We can come with absolutely nothing but emptiness, humility, and an open hand to draw from a well that is endless in godly wisdom, creativity, and power. What he supplies us with might not be what we expected or anticipated, but we can trust that it's good and it's what we need.

Friends, there is no error in our design. While my list of inadequacies is probably different than yours, I'd be willing to bet that our conclusion is probably the same: what I've got is not enough. And that confession is not falsehood; it's freedom. We are not enough in and of ourselves because we were designed for a partnership—Christ in us and united with the Holy Spirit. Being tethered to Christ and his Spirit isn't a restraint; it's our greatest strength.

Free to Need Others

Part of being a new creation in Christ means we not only walk in Spirit-reliance instead of self-reliance, but we are also called into a community of believers on whom we can rely too. In 1 Corinthians 12:27, Paul refers to the people of God as the body of Christ, and each one of us is a part of it. As believers, we all share in the same Spirit. Remember? It's not just Christ in you, it's Christ in y'all. We aren't called to a life of just "me and Jesus." Rather, we are called to be united with Christ and his body. We aren't invited into a life of just needing him, but also being okay with needing each other.

When we're caught up in living lives of striving and self-sufficiency, we are less likely to invite others into these places of inadequacy, insecurity, or into our struggles with sin because we believe we're enough to handle it. Community requires humility and the confession: "I can't do this alone, and I need people to come around me and hold me up." Striving forces us to keep on a mask and keep people out of our business. But friends, what precious gifts we refuse when we don't let people in! The truth is, we can experience and receive the love, encouragement, and grace that Christ offers us through another believer, because Christ is in them, equipping them to encourage us. When we hold believers at arm's length, keep our mess to ourselves, and act like we have it all together, we resist receiving the love of Christ through another person. We miss out when we refuse to need others.

In my early twenties, I was invited to a women's small group by a sweet friend I had just made, Nicole. I made up excuses why I couldn't go every week, but this girl did not stop! Eventually, I caved. My first Saturday, I sat back with my jaw on the floor at the things these women were confessing to each other. I mean, they were *layin' their junk* out there—all of it. Although my cheeks were burning red with disbelief, my heart was stirred and encouraged, because after they got it all out, they rallied around each other. They prayed for each other and spoke straight truth to tough situations and valid feelings. If there was a need, whether material or spiritual, these ladies rallied again, funded families, and shared what they had. Each week, they asked about each other's progress and shared their breakthroughs and breakdowns. They were truly invested in one another's lives. They lived needy. A couple months in, I finally had the guts to start sharing my junk too, and

I had never experienced a relief like that. I had never allowed a community of people carry my struggles before. This was such a great example for me to see the spirit of Christ in other believers admonishing, encouraging, and pouring into other souls. It was like receiving grace from God himself through one of his kids. This was my first invitation into rich community that practices needing each other.

I see it this way: as we plant our lives on the foundation of Christ—our steady stream of living water—we abide in him by sending our roots down into him. Our nourishment, sustenance, and help come from him **first**. He is our ultimate sustainer. However, as believers, it is so important that we plant our lives both in Christ and *beside* one another. We live dependent on God and also on one another.

As I was on a walk one day, I was asking God to show me what this kind of relationship with others looks like. As I made my way around my neighborhood, a picture of two uprooted trees came to my mind. Because they were uprooted, I could see the root system clearly. It was the strangest thing—the roots of these two trees were all tangled up and wrapped tightly around one another. Once I got home, I started researching what kinds of trees intertwine their roots with the tree next to them. I couldn't believe what I found! Once again, through his creation, God gives us a physical demonstration of what this type of dependence looks like through a tree called the Tabonuco.

Tangled Roots

Deep in the heart of Puerto Rico, there is a species of tree that dwells in clusters among the ridges and slopes of major forests. They are a slow growing tree because it takes time to develop their incredibly strong root systems. Among all the trees in the rain forest, time and time again, this particular type of tree is the one to withstand the harsh hurricanes that happen there. Why? Because of its surrounding community.

One of the most impressive things about Tabonucos is that as they are growing, they will start intertwining their roots with the Tabonucos next to them, securing their roots around each other in groups of ten to twenty trees.[1] While most trees tend to be uprooted during a hurricane, this tree will lose its leaves and branches, but the roots stay firm and intact because they are anchored in one another. In a hurricane, something must give, and it will typically be the weakest part of the structure: the roots, the trunk, or the leaves. With each hurricane, it becomes more and more clear that the Tabonuco's interconnected roots are its strength.

One reporter said that right after Hurricane Maria, he went to a Tabonuco saturated forest and said it was totally brown because of the destruction and loss of leaves.[2] However, he returned in six months and those same trees were covered in green leaves again. They were able to recover quickly because not only do their roots keep them anchored in a storm, but the tangled Tabonucos also share nutrients with one another.[3] This helps them recover their crowns and leaves quickly. Researchers also found that hurricane damage was significantly higher in isolated Tabonucos than in those in unions.[4] Even God's creation proclaims his brilliant design—we are made to send our roots down into God's stream of living water and wrap our roots around each other.

Is this not the most beautiful picture of what a community of believers could look like? When we plant our lives in community next to other abiding believers, we can send our roots not just into the stream of living water, but we can also entwine and entangle our roots with those next to us. Just like the Tabonuco network, we can be a part of an interdependent community that shares a power source and nutrients, acts as anchors in a storm, and together provides a safe shelter for those who need rest from a hard world.

This is what community with Christ and one another looks like. Jesus has liberated us from a life of *me* into a life of *need*. We were purposefully designed to need God and each other, and guess what. We actually flourish in our need. God's Word and even his creation makes it painstakingly clear: being tethered in need to Christ and his body isn't restraint; it's our greatest strength.

EXPERIENCING FREEDOM GUIDE

Reflect

Self-reliance has been one of the greatest, most unsuspecting enemies to the gospel. When we live lives that say, "I can make it through with what I've got," it eliminates the need for the Holy Spirit and other believers. We live our lives in these salt-ridden lands because we think we have everything within ourselves to get us through what we need. But because of the gospel, we have nothing to prove to ourselves, anyone else, or even to God. He has freed us to need, rely, and depend on the Holy Spirit and others. We can not only draw near to God, seeking to know him more, as a personal pursuit; we can also grow in our knowledge of God by running alongside other Christ-followers. When we are free to need others, this allows us to experience Christ's love in a deeper way. How would our daily lives change if we lived aware of our need and made a lifestyle of running to the Giver again and again and again?

Journal

1. Do you feel like you run to the Holy Spirit for your needs? What would it look like to make a practice of turning to him when you come up against inadequacy, insecurity, or a struggle with temptation and sin?

_____

_____

_____

_____

2. How would you describe your current community situation? Does your community *know* you? Do you *know* them? What would you like your community to look like?

_____

_____

_____

_____

_____

_____

Write It & Memorize It

"Let us then with confidence draw near to the throne of grace, that we may receive mercy and find grace to help in time of need." —Hebrews 4:16 (ESV)

"And my God will supply every need of yours according to his riches in glory in Christ Jesus." —Philippians 4:19 (ESV)

Call to Action

Do you want your community to be more vulnerable with each other? Go first. Do you desire it to be more spiritually connected? Start a text group and talk about what you're learning and need prayer for throughout the week. Don't have a community? Get plugged into a small group or create your own!

Notes

[1] Ariel E. Lugo and Frank H. Wadsworth, "*Dacryodes excelsa* Vahl," accessed July 16, 2021, https://www.srs.fs.usda.gov/pubs/misc/ag_654/volume_2/dacryodes/excelsa.htm.

[2] Stephen Long, "The Puerto Rican Trees That Can Stand Up to Hurricanes," Zócalo Public Square, July 17, 2018, https://www.zocalopublicsquare.org/2018/07/17/puerto-rican-trees-can-stand-hurricanes/ideas/essay/.

[3] Amber Dance, "How Trees Fare in Big Hurricanes," *The Scientist*, February 1, 2019, https://www.the-scientist.com/features/how-trees-fare-in-big-hurricanes-65335.

[4] Khadga Basnet, F. N. Scatena, Gene E. Likens, and Ariel E. Lugo, "Ecological Consequences of Root Grafting in Tabonuco (*Dacryodes excelsa*) Trees in the Luquillo Experimental Forest, Puerto Rico," *Biotropica* 25, no. 1 (1993): 28–35. doi:10.2307/2388976.

Chapter Fourteen

FREE TO SET OTHERS FREE

I have no problem admitting that I've had a very complicated relationship with the word "evangelism." For years, evangelism looked like memorizing a four-part monologue, analyzing a person's story to see where I could squeeze Jesus in, and either feeling relief in being able to tell my ministry leader that I shared the gospel that week or overwhelming guilt if I didn't. While I was so thankful to have received training and practice in evangelism, I had yet again morphed telling people about Jesus into something I had to do to keep God and me on good terms.

Throughout my early twenties, the ministry I was involved in made regular practice of getting out in our city and evangelizing. I faithfully used my memorized script to tell people about Jesus, but my motivations were completely fear-based because I thought that in my doing this, I was maintaining God's approval and acceptance. What's worse, in my effort to check the "I told someone about Jesus" box, I reduced real people with real hearts and stories into checkmarks. I didn't care about them or their eternity. I didn't care enough to listen to their story. I just wanted to tell my four-part monologue and throw the offer to accept Jesus out there so I could check a box for my own perceived gain. (Now, could God still use the script to lead people to him? Of course. The power of the gospel isn't dependent on my performance—it is power all in itself.) But as I shared, I did not feel free to tell the story of Jesus, I felt forced. How is it possible to feel guilt, shame, pride, and self-assurance all at the mention of one word: "evangelism"?

My complicated relationship with evangelism came to a head during a mission trip to South Padre Island during Spring Break. This particular mission trip was aimed at reaching college students with the gospel by offering free rides across the island, talking with people on the beach, and working at a pop-up pancake shop in the early hours of the morning. Three days into the trip, I felt so overwhelmed with the pressure to present the story of Jesus quickly, to tell it perfectly, and to check off the evangelism box that I eventually snapped—and I'm so glad I did. At 3 a.m. in the church van, I yelled to my team, "I just can't do this! I'm done!" and started crying. At that moment, I felt I had deeply disappointed God, failed as a follower, and had no business being there. While my team assured me the discouragement was okay, something inside me had become so dissatisfied with this way of thinking and doing things that I gave up. I was done with this trip, and I was done trying to do what I originally went there to do—rather, went there to prove. Yet, a rejection of the old way of doing things was the perfect segue for the Holy Spirit to show me a new way of doing things—of how to tell from a place of freedom instead of fear. This way led me to rely on him, to see people the way he saw them, and to tell others about him from a place of being free.

The next morning, our group leader announced that we would be splitting up into groups of two and going to talk to people all across the island. I had already made up my mind that I would not be doing any talking, so my partner would just have to be okay with doing it all. My frustration level rose to a whole new level when we got our assignment: we would be splitting from our partner and talking to people inside an IHOP. I remember thinking, "Really? You want me to interrupt people's breakfast and ask if I can tell them about Jesus real quick? Should I ask to sit at their table?! Or ask for a bite of their pancakes?!" As you can see, I did not want to be there. But as I walked through the doors, I felt the Lord impress on my heart, "Can I show you a different way of telling? Will you follow me, and let me lead you?" Although I was incredibly reluctant, I said yes. While I looked around the very crowded dining room, two girls in a corner booth stuck out to me, one of them chowing down on her pancakes, and one ranting to a friend on the phone. In that moment, I felt a strong leading to walk over to their table.

I honestly don't even remember what I said when I approached them. All I remember is that within five minutes of me offering the pancake eater a free ride and asking what she did for a living, she broke down in tears. She went on to tell me that she was interning as a party planner on the island and felt like her heart was in the darkest place it had ever been. At that moment, I said, "Can I sit with you and hear more?" She said yes.

As she told me her story, the Lord opened my eyes to see her heart. I could feel her discouragement, her fear of being too far for God to love her, and the deep desire for her heart to be rescued out of this dark place. For the first time, I could see the heart in front of me. When she finished, I was able to tell her about who Jesus is, what he did for her, and how he could set her free. I was able to share about how he met me intimately in a very dark place in my own life. I told her about how his love had radically pursued me and allowed me to feel so dissatisfied with the way I was living that I had no other option than to run to him. I remember this woman,

Megan, telling me she wanted a relationship with him, and I was happy to tell her she could respond to that call into a relationship herself, and she did.

The most hilarious part of this whole story is that during the entire duration of this conversation, Megan's friend (remember the other girl at the table?) was *still* on the phone! She kept intermittently mouthing to Megan, "What the #$%# is happening right now? What are you crying about? Do you even know this girl?" Nevertheless, we kept on talking. We prayed together, cried together, and forty-five minutes later, I left the table and cried again at what God had done not just in her life, but what he had done in mine.

For the first time, I felt free to tell—not out of fear but from freedom. In talking about the ways God set me free, I was able to point somebody else to the author of freedom and watch God set her free too. This is what we **get** to do! This is our greatest call and the mission Jesus left us with—go and tell. Christ has radically set us free so we can show others the way to freedom and watch them get set free too. But you wanna know the most effective way to get a free person to shut up and not share anything at all? Get them to be so ridden with fear that they'll never move their feet—or their mouth.

When Fear Barks, Bite Back

Fear is the great paralyzer and a truly awful motivator. When fear drives our lives, especially our obedience to God, we will end up eyeing our performance and how we are doing instead of looking at Christ, his sufficiency, and how he can help us do what he's called us to. When it comes to sharing our stories and talking about what God has done, fear will make us hyperfocused on getting every word right, on presenting everything perfectly, and on thoughts like . . .

- What if I'm not understood?
- What if they reject me?
- What if I'm asked a question I don't know?
- What if I explain Jesus incorrectly and sound confusing?
- What if I turn them off Jesus and make things even worse?
- What if I do it all wrong?

In combination with all these fears, I was personally afraid that if I didn't share the gospel every day, God would be mad or disappointed in me. It felt like a "have to" rooted in fear, and not a "get to" rooted in freedom. I felt both motivated and paralyzed by that same fear. It both motivated me to act out of fear of punishment and paralyzed me from doing anything at all! Instead of being mobilized, I felt trapped in analysis paralysis—obsessing over whether what I had to say was good enough, polished enough, or intelligent enough.

But one important thing that fear forgets to mention is that as we tell, we have the Spirit in us, leading, guiding, and giving words to us as we minister. He isn't up in the sky with a rating scale ready to judge how effective our "gospel presentation" was. Remember—Christ is in us. He is right in the middle of the field equipping, empowering, and giving boldness to our hearts as we proclaim freedom to the person right in front of us. Not to mention, the Spirit is the one who softens hearts, draws all people to Christ, and does the heart work. We don't! This takes the pressure off us to perform perfectly and invites us into a deep dependence on the Spirit. When we don't know how to tell our stories, what to say, or how to respond, we can ask him for wisdom, pray for what to say next, and he is faithful to help us. Recently, I've found myself praying, "Lord, remove this shadow of fear over me, and instead, may you overshadow me in this moment. Show me what this person needs to hear and give me the boldness to say and do it."

When fear paralyzes our mouths from declaring the freedom that is available to others, we can remind ourselves:

- My righteousness before God isn't dependent on what I do; it is solely because of Christ.
- Performance isn't my priority, dependence is.
- I can daily ask the Holy Spirit to lead me to people and ask for his help in what to say.
- It's okay if my speech and my telling are imperfect because it is the power of God that sets people free and draws people to himself, not me.
- A spirit of fear has no place in me because I've been given a spirit of power, love, and a sound mind.

Therefore, I am free to show up and I am free to tell because . . .

- I am loved by God, not based on how I perform.
- I am confident in the work of Christ.
- The Spirit of Christ is *in* me, and I can trust him to lead me in this moment and all those to come.
- Christ's heart is centered on setting people free, so I will be about what he is about.

The Sword of Your Story

One of the most powerful ways we can tell people about Christ is by telling them about what he has done for us. I want to invite you to pause and consider the ways God has specifically set you free—whether it be in tiny victories from ten months ago or major breakthroughs from ten years ago. Think about all the ways you felt trapped, unable to change, and confident that things would never turn around for you.

How did Jesus intercept your story? How did he change your heart, break chains from your wrists, free you from striving, heal your heart, and set your feet to run free again? How did he show himself faithful when you just wanted to quit him? How did he unravel lies and renew your mind over time? When did you start to notice that you didn't operate in the same ways you used to? How did your heart respond? How did the way you live radically change?

You, my friend, are a firsthand witness to receiving the miraculous freedom of Jesus Christ and his Spirit. When we sit back and think about the ways God has freed us and how he's moved in our stories, it reignites this flame in us that can be easily dimmed by a cynical world, tough circumstances, and our own self-doubt. May we never forget the ways we've been set free. Because when we lose sight of the unbelievable ways Jesus has set us free, we'll inevitably become less concerned with the freedom of others. When we make a habit of remembering the ways we've been set free, we remain convinced of the crazy power of God, and we go into situations with our eyes set on that confidence instead of placing it in ourselves.

When we look at stories like the woman at the well, the man who was freed from demons, and the man Jesus healed from being deaf and mute, we see that once Jesus set them free, they ran back to their places and told the story of how this man, Jesus, set them free. In response to their stories, the hearers flocked to Jesus. Not because of the way these people eloquently talked about Jesus, asked good questions, or gave powerful monologues—it was because these people experienced the power of God in their stories. The point of their telling was not that people would look at them, but that people would be amazed at what happened and go find Christ. The way we tell should be no different. The banner of our lives should be: "Look at this Man who set me free! He can do it for you, too!"

Your story of freedom is like a sword in your sheath and a torch in your hand. Scripture says we overcome the enemy by two things: by the blood of the Lamb (what Jesus has done) and by the word of our testimony (what we've witnessed God do) (Rev. 12:11). The enemy's plan is that no one would look at or come to Christ; that they would instead look to themselves and remain in patterns of constant hopelessness. But our stories of what God has done act as a weapon to combat the lies and the plan of the enemy because they point to a Savior who is in the here and now. We have proof because we've experienced it firsthand. Our freedom stories are also a torch. In the midst of a dark world, the Lord has personally and corporately encountered us and given us the Light of the World, the fire of the Spirit, to guide us. This light not only leads us, but also draws other people to the light, and we can tell others exactly how to receive it. Our stories are an invitation to others to hear about the greatest news of all time, how we witnessed this freedom personally, and how they can be set free too.

Life on Fire

Where striving kept us paralyzed in fear, freedom has released our feet to run wild with this story of grace. It has set our life on fire that we may be a light to the world and ultimately point them to Jesus with our lives.

Mr. Charles is a very special man in my life who constantly teaches me what "life on fire" looks like. I don't know if I've ever met anyone who is freer, whose feet are less stunted by fear, whose speech is less paralyzed by perfectionism. He introduces the light of Christ to the unbeliever, and he is an energetic fan to the flame inside his brothers and sisters in Christ. I wish everyone could meet him. When I asked Mr. Charles what it looks like to walk fearlessly in telling the story of God, he explained that he finds freedom when his eyes come off himself and he instead places them on Christ. Because when his eyes aren't fixated on the fear of rejection, what people will say, or how they will respond, he is able to see the heart of Christ, who is passionate about people coming to know and experience him.

Striving for a perfect performance and hyperfixation on the opinions of others has kept our feet paralyzed and our tongues tied from telling the story of God. Friend, we have been set free to set others free! We are representatives of Christ, ambassadors of freedom with a story to tell about what he has done. Your story, no matter how insignificant it seems or how insecure you feel about it, can be a weapon used to break barriers that keep people stuck. Your testimony can invite others into a relationship with Christ and light a fire in someone's heart to run radically free.

So, with your torch in hand, let your eyes become fixed on the fire Christ has lit for you. And with all the confidence placed solely on the Spirit inside you and the reasons for your freedom placed on the person of Christ, run wild. Light fires, get loud, and make a mess of the world in front of you for the sake of Christ. Don't be afraid to surrender the ordinary, mundane days before our Father in heaven and ask how he wants to light a fire in your midst today. With our eyes set on Jesus, let's fearlessly raise these torches of freedom in our day jobs, in our homes, in the classroom, during an Uber drive across town, at the coffee shop, in our churches, in the grocery store, and in the carpool line.

As we walk through our everyday lives, I want to challenge us to get in line with the agenda of the Spirit of God and ask him to lead us there. You never know, he might lead you to the girl in IHOP who needs to know that God loves her. Or to the young woman who is desperate for godly leadership and mentorship in her life. Perhaps to the child in your house who is battling fear and needs to know about the peace of God. He might move you to strike conversation in your normal, everyday activities. Who knows! Let's make his business about freedom our business.

Lord, we are yours. Give us a fresh revelation of your heart and desire for people. Help us to be as passionate about people's freedom as you are. Thank you for setting us free so that we may lead other people to the author of freedom.

EXPERIENCING FREEDOM GUIDE

Reflect

Once we've tasted the freedom that comes from knowing Christ, we cannot help but share that fire with others. Yet fear, insecurity, and even guilt can warp what is supposed to be a bold declaration about Christ into something we stay silent about. The beautiful thing is that Christ in us gives us the words, power, and boldness to tell others about him and the freedom he offers us. In moments when we are tempted to back down, the Spirit in us helps us stand tall and tell others about freedom in Christ so they may find freedom too.

Journal

1. What has been your experience when it comes to sharing your faith? Do you find yourself stepping out in boldness or shrinking back in fear?

_____

_____

_____

_____

2. Whom has God strategically placed in your life to share your story of freedom with? Whom has God burdened your heart for?

_____

_____

_____

_____

_____

_____

Write It & Memorize It

"Out of my distress I called on the LORD; the LORD answered me and set me free." —Psalm 118:5 (ESV)

"The Spirit of the Lord GOD is upon me, because the LORD has anointed me to bring good news to the poor; he has sent me to bind up the brokenhearted, to proclaim liberty to the captives, and the opening of the prison to those who are bound." —Isaiah 61:1 (ESV)

Call to Action

I've found that the Lord often places people in our path who need to hear the truth about him or experience his love through us. Think about whom those people might be in your life. Perhaps they could be the people you work with, the woman you see at the coffee shop every Tuesday, the teenager who reluctantly comes to church with her mom, or another person who has stuck out to you. Commit to praying for that person this week and asking God to provide an opportunity to be a blessing to them, to meet with them, or share your story with them.

Chapter Fifteen

FREE TO COME CLOSE

Once we become aware of God's amazing gifts, his love, and the freedom he offers, our first inclination might be to immediately get to work and start working for God. We're ready to sign up, say, "Put me in coach!" and go accomplish things for him. And yet, I believe there is still another area he longs for us to find freedom in. Rather than running out to be a witness from a distance, it may be that God is beckoning us to draw closer to him. Perhaps this might just be what his heart longs for the most. We are not just free to come to him; we are free to come close.

Of all the relationships God could have chosen to have with the people he made, he chose an intimate, dependent relationship. He didn't make obedient robots without a will, or perfect people who would serve him on a professional level. He didn't simply create beautiful statues that looked pretty and didn't have hearts, wills, or unruly emotions. No. Instead he chose, perhaps, the most tender, interactive, loving, dependent, and dare I say messiest relationship possible: **He chose for us to be his kids.** And is not the heart of a Father for his kids to love him, embrace him, tell him where it hurts, and let him pour life, love, and purpose into them? Of all the things a Father could desire, would it not be for his children to trust him enough to come close?

Personally, my dad has modeled the overwhelming, supportive, break-down-doors-to-comfort-me kind of love for all my life. I have story after story of God showing me how he loves through my own earthly father. But I do realize for some, viewing God as a Father might feel terrifying or uncomfortable. Maybe you had a father who walked away, took love away more than he gave it, who wanted to be right more than he wanted you to feel safe, stripped you of value, or made you run for his affection instead of assuring you that you belonged. Can I interject for a second and tell you: our Father in heaven—his love is not broken. It is not selfish. It hasn't been tainted with pride, fear, or insecurity. He is the author of love, and he invented the role of a Father. His love is completely incomparable and greater than the love of even the best, most caring earthly father. He Fathers us with a love so divine that it not only transforms us, but it also satisfies the deepest places of our soul.

Of all the things he could've been for us, he made himself a haven. A safe place for his children to come freely and be reminded, "I made you. I am wild about you. I know you best, and I know what is best **for** you. I am not going to take my love away from you because you failed. You can trust me—I am good." This is the love we've been looking for all along. The best news is that we don't have to earn it, run for it, perform to receive it, or prove why we're good enough to have it. It's ours. And he wants us to come close and receive it all the days of our lives.

The Broken Veil

The Old Testament talks about a time when the presence of God rested behind the veil in the Holy of Holies in the Tabernacle. This sacred space was accessible only under certain conditions, by certain priests, and after the most thorough preparations had been made. But on the day Jesus died, as he took his last breath, the veil that separated the presence of God from the people of God was physically ripped in two. Almost as if God himself declared, "No more!"

No more separation.

No more preparation.

The very sin that separated us was taken upon the back of God's Son, who laid his life down that we may be rescued; our relationship with the Father was restored so we could come home and come close. Jesus became the door by which we could enter freely (John 10:9), that through belief in him, we could walk freely into the presence of God. We have been given an access pass, that was bought with a life, that lets us come right in, day or night.

This is a gift like no other—this was the design all along. Coming close is God's design from the beginning, is it not? In the garden we see that nothing was hidden—nothing in all creation. Everything was exposed to be enjoyed and beheld intimately. God and humanity walked together with nothing standing in the way. Where sin made coming close impossible, God sent his only Son to bridge the gap. Breaking his own heart and body, he made a way to come close again.

Oh, what we're missing when we believe we can't come, that we must clean up to come, or that we can only come to him at a distance. We've believed that we have to justify our way into his presence, and we've let failure keep us out. Could it be that striving has been the greatest distraction from us coming close to the Father?

Striving has kept us professional.

It's made time with God a duty and a box to be checked.

In trying to prove, we lose sight of his love, and we don't feel the need to linger in his presence.

Our own inadequacy has convinced us to stay at a distance and miss the gift of intimate delight.

I'm convinced that the enemy has filled our minds with aromas of amnesia to make us forget the torn veil and make us think we have to run for an access we already have. He aims to keep us running for love instead of returning to the Father who can remind us we already are loved. Friends, there is power when we are free to come close.

Because everything changes when we do.

The Father's House

I'm going to invite you into my brain (don't mind the mess) and paint you a picture that has completely changed this idea of intimacy with God. Lately when I pray, sit down to read my Bible, or just enjoy time with God, I envision myself walking in the dark of the morning up to the front door of a big house. I'm coming because I just want to see God, be with him, and listen to him. And when I come, there aren't any guards at the door because I have access. I am his kid. I've been given keys and can come boldly before him. When I come through the door, he calls me to come close. To come in the study and sit right beside him where the fire's warm. In my mind, this is what I envision when I think about coming close to God—to have the kind of access a child has.

This kind of childlike freedom is ultimately an act of trust. It's believing that everything that's been done for a restored relationship is finished, that I truly am a child of God, and that I can come boldly before the throne of grace. When we experience this kind of childlike freedom to come near him, we find ourselves in a trust-infused, intimate relationship with our Creator that is unlike anything we've experienced before. We find that all striving ceases because our eyes are looking at a Father who has no needs, who simply just wants us and invites us. Our hearts are richly fulfilled when we let him lavish us with a love that satisfies a thousand dreams; a love that is a balm to a broken heart, tends to our hurting wounds, and reminds us that we cannot see all things like he does. Through his Word, he reminds us of his heart and once again invites us to trust him. When we find ourselves off track and flirting with immaturity, he tells us, "Child, this is ill-fitting on you and will hurt you—let me show you a better way," and we receive that correction in trust.

Better yet, we find ourselves not just pouring out our hearts and issues before him, but we begin listening to his heart. Our hearts begin to break as we see his heart break over lost ones who believe they can't come, can't return, or are hesitant to return—convinced there is nothing that will make them worthy enough to walk through those doors. We listen as he tells us what he is doing all around the world, in believers and unbelievers alike. The wonders of what he is doing gets us fired up, and he asks us to be apart—to join him in what he's doing, assuring us that he'll help, guide, and lead us. It's his work and his vision, after all. During those times we doubt and wrestle with his invitation, he reminds us what we were actually made for; revealing the gifts, talents, and personality traits that he specifically gave to us so that people might know him. He tells us how to use them, and in trust, we walk those things out.

The crazy part is the more we come close, we'll notice that we start talking like him. We begin thinking like him, seeing people the same way he does, and our hearts start to break like his does. After all, we tend to become like those we hang around the most, yes? People start coming into our path who have no clue about the Father's house, and we feel internally compelled to tell them. We do all we can to lead them there, because we know there is nothing like it because there is nothing like him. Our lives suddenly become about getting people to know him and telling them they are free to come close.

As we live, we find that all our ministry, devotion, obedience to the Father, and love for him comes from this sacred place, from this freedom to come close. Who knew that such freedom could come when we trust him enough to draw near? This act of intimacy is rebellion against striving; it is abiding in every sense of the word. It is fully embracing the identity of a child of the living God and walking in agreement with that identity in every single area of life.

The Sweetest Invitation

Sometimes I reflect on this and think: *There is no way this can be true*. There is something innate in me that believes I've got to run for something, strive for what I want, and that really great things only come to those who work their tails off for it.

Trusting God has been the biggest, scariest response of my life. A life of striving has proven to be a lot more controlled, more measurable, more comfortable, and therefore I'm tempted to choose that way of living so many times. Trusting the work of Christ and the love of the Father often feels like a dare to go skydiving—flying ten thousand feet in the air only to jump out of a plane with some dude strapped to your back. In this spiritual freefall, you trust him when he says "Jump!" You trust him when the hard ground below you is coming fast and you're hoping like mad that the parachute will catch you. You are greatly relieved when it does, in fact, catch you. You trust him when he says, "Open your eyes!" and you're left floating in the sky, overlooking the most gorgeous scenery that you would never have experienced unless you were risky enough to jump out of that plane. In the same way, Christ invites us to respond to him in trust, and it takes us to places we never could have experienced unless we decided to take the risk and believe him.

As you walk a life of belief and trust, you'll be a firsthand witness to the pressure falling from your shoulders—because life isn't about **you** anymore. The incessant need to prove yourself dissipates as you grow more and more convinced that what your Father says is truer than anything else. The need to strive for love dissolves as you regularly let him love you and you receive his love. You stop chasing the idea of being "good enough" because you've found that he is more than enough, and realize he is in you. This is what freedom looks like, sounds like, and feels like. And it's yours in Christ, friend. You have full permission to step off the hamster wheel and plant your feet on the security of Christ, and watch as he sets you drastically free.

The invitation at the beginning of this book was for those working in the fields to come back home as sons, and yet, there is one more invitation I believe the Father makes available to us today.

Will we trust him enough to come close?

Will we believe that there is nothing that separates us from him—not our failure, not our brokenness, not our striving, not our past? Will we take full assurance that there is not a secret password to come into his presence and that Jesus is the door by which we enter freely? That through his sacrifice we've been given a costly ID badge that gives us unlimited access to the Creator of the universe—our Father? Will we choose to believe that he loves it when we come?

I penned these words in my journal one day as an invitation and response for myself, and I want to share them with you:

Where the power of sin disrupted intimacy and sealed off the heavenly door,
Our Savior became the mediator; that separation would be no more.

If there is no separation, and there's nothing left that needs to be done,
In the full assurance of Jesus, do you realize—you're free to come?

Will you come close on both the mountaintop and on days your knees hit the floor?
When you feel more stuck than you've ever felt, or just can't take it anymore?
Will you come when you feel anxious? When you simply want to escape?
Will you let his love embrace you—let his hands cup your face?

Do you trust that he won't look away when you fail or get off track?
That his kindness leads to repentance; that his love will lead you back?
Do you believe you can come whenever, not just when you're "good"?
That you can bare your soul before him and never leave misunderstood?

Mark up your walls with this reminder—let it never leave your sight:
We've been given access to the Father, who bids us come, day or night.
We can come close in our obedience, in our failure and indifference,
Our hearts assured in the love of God and there—we place our confidence.

> So go on—walk up the steps and crack open the front door.
> You're free to trust.
> Free to come close.
> This is where it all changes—you'll see.

EXPERIENCING FREEDOM GUIDE

Reflect

Aren't you thankful we serve a God who invites us close to his heart? To draw near in any season of our life? I often find myself so busy doing things "for God" that I forget I was made to be in constant connection and community with God, spending time with him and resting in his presence. Do you find yourself in a similar pattern? Do you feel the freedom to come close to the heart of the Father?

Journal

1. What is your initial response to the statement that we are free to come close to God? Does this statement cause feelings of initial resistance or relief? Why do you think that is?

   _____

   _____

   _____

   _____

   _____

2. What would it look like for your time with God to be less about checking off a box and more about enjoying his presence, listening, responding, and being with him?

   _____

   _____

_____

_____

_____

_____

Write It & Memorize It

"My heart has heard you say, 'Come and talk with me.' And my heart responds, 'Lord, I am coming.'"
—Psalm 27:8 (NLT)

"For you have been my help, and in the shadow of your wings I will sing for joy. My soul clings to you; your right hand upholds me." —Psalm 63:7–8 (ESV)

Call to Action

Schedule some time this week to get out of the house and spend time with God in an inconspicuous place. This might look like going to a coffee shop, getting outdoors in nature, going to your favorite spot in town, or even just stepping into your backyard to spend time with him. Bring your Bible and journal, grab your guitar if you have one, and spend this time simply being with him. Let him know what's on your heart and listen to him speak to you—all for the sake of enjoying being with him.

Final Thoughts

FREE TO RUN

Can you see it?

Miles and miles of lush, green grass before you. The wind blowing through your hair. You take a deep breath—the air feels so good as it fills up your lungs. Go ahead—kick your shoes off—you are free to run wild in this wide-open field called grace.

It's a whole new world out here.

You won't find hamster wheels, measuring sticks, glass cases filled with your hard-won trophies or well-deserved demerits. You can't bring anything with you here. There aren't even notepads out here in this place—lest you be tempted to start making checklists again. I've had to find new hobbies, as there aren't any mirages out here to chase—mirages that held false promises of all the ways I could finally be enough. I never could quite catch them, but I sure got tired trying. Instead, this field is saturated with streams of real, living water that promise to satisfy—and they do. It is actually enough and quenches the desire to be enough. Feast on this stuff long enough and your thirst for the world just dissipates.

And the people! Oh, the people, they are radically different. They aren't in competition with one another but rather dwell in rich, authentic community. It's no utopia—it's messy and people still wound one another, but they refuse to let bitterness stay. They forgive, confess, and stay honest with each other, depending on one another as they depend on the Father. Their love for each other has been modeled by the author of love.

I just know you'll love it here, and my prayer is that you'll only return to the deserts of striving to lead the wanderers here—to this place called grace. Their feet are tired from walking miles, only to drink dirty water from broken cisterns they dug themselves. They're exhausted from chasing mirages of "enough" and their souls can't find real rest. They often live alone or around those who fend for themselves. They compete for food and shade. This desert life of striving has them malnourished, sunburned, and desperate for more. I'm so thankful someone showed me a way out, and I encourage you to show others the better way. Remind them of the Good Story—again. Tell them how they're free. Remind them of the God of grace and of this field that is available for them to come close and run free.

Dear reader, I have thought of you and prayed for you for such a long time now. I've beckoned for our God to totally wreck your world with his grace—that you would never walk the same. I've asked that he would release your feet to run. I wish I could sit across from you and hear the stories of how he's set you free from a life of striving for acceptance and met you with his love. Maybe someday, we will be able to do that.

So, friend, with feet fitted with the gospel of peace, run. With love in your heart and assurance in your spirit, run with the One who sets souls free. Do what he created you to do. Scatter seeds like a mad person, trusting that it is he who makes things grow in his time. Tune your heart to hear him say, "Go here!" or "Go there!" because he will faithfully lead you to hearts that need his touch. Fearlessly go and light up your places—no matter how mundane or ordinary they may feel. You'll be amazed at what God can do when we trust him and just give him our "yes."

May your love for the Father grow deeper and deeper as you trust him more and more. You'll find obedience and surrender come quicker because your confidence in his goodness is changing. Enjoy his presence, friend. It's a gift—the delight of our lives.

And on those days when failure is loud, when you feel messy and the need to prove is so overwhelmingly strong, remember your new identity and voice your trust to the One who is maturing you. You can even ask him to help you trust him.

Because you are free to grow.

Free to fail and get back up.

Free to admit that you don't have this and that you need help.

Free to lean on God and other people.

Free to confess when you get it wrong.

Let all these beautiful realities remind you that you are free to run—without hindrance, shame, shackles, or heavy weights. You are free to live wild, running unchained in these fields of grace. The Son has set you free, so for goodness' sake, go be free.

I'm joyfully and wildly cheering you on from across the field.

Kaitlin

ACKNOWLEDGMENTS

This book has been one of the most unexpected gifts of my life. I wish I could tell you every little detail of how this book came to be, because I will surely remember the goodness of God weaved through it all. As I wrote this book, I not only experienced God's provision in the words to write, but also in the people he surrounded me with who truly made this happen. I am indebted to the amazing tribe who listened to my fears and spoke truth until those fears were silenced, for the random phone calls, brainstorm sessions, hours spent reading my choppy rough drafts, and to the amazing team of publishers, editors, and ministries who took a chance on me. I am so thankful for each one of you.

God: This is all your fault . . . ☺ You made a way when I didn't think there could ever be one. You breathed life into a dormant dream. Thank you for pursuing my heart and setting it free, time and time again. Learning about grace and how to receive your love has been the most incredible journey. Thank you for your provision and extravagance in all the intricate details that only you and I know—you know me in ways I will never get over.

Lance: Gosh, I love you. You made so many sacrifices to make this book happen, and I am so thankful for each one of them. You've been the loudest, most excited cheerleader from the time this book was just a random thought, and you've been cheering it on like a wild man the whole way through. Your encouragement fires me up and fuels me.

Dad: I would have never written this book had it not been for your one-thousand pep talks to "put my big girl panties on" and do hard things even if I'm scared out of my mind. Your brave voice has been in my head as I wrote each page. Your words and analogies are scattered all through this book. I love you.

Mom: I'm pretty sure this book was written on the backbone of your prayers. You have been a haven for me: you've supported me, encouraged me, prayed over me countless times, and your Oxford comma is stamped on every page. You are so precious to me. I love us, and I love you.

Kaden: You are my longest, dearest friend, and I will never stop being over-the-moon proud of you. Thank you for always cheering me on, telling me to toughen up and trust God, and for believing in this dream even before I did. I love you so much.

Bart and Arlene: I don't know how in the world I got so lucky to have the greatest in-loves in the whole world. You have supported my writing from the very beginning, let me hone the craft of writing in the office all those years, and have been such an encouragement and comfort to me. I love you both so very much.

To my enormous Hoyt/Kirkpatrick/Garrison/Greaser tribe of grandparents, aunts, uncles, and cousins: I seriously have the best family in the world. Thank you for your countless prayers, encouraging texts and calls, and for rooting me on.

To my friends, for whom I am eternally grateful: God has blessed me with friendships I do not remotely deserve. You have watched this story play out in my life and have held my hands up as I've written this book. Joanna, Maurissa, Taylor, Abigail, Nazsoni, Mary, Emily, Trish—thank you for loving me well, leading me kindly, forcing me to have fun (hehe!), and pointing me back to Jesus. I will never get over God's kindness in giving you to me.

YAM Fam: You are the earth's greatest small group. You guys are family. Thank you for doing life with me and for being the best cheerleaders, supporters, and life-giving friends.

TWC Church Staff and Family: I love our church so much. Thank you for being a tribe of people that points me back to truth and provides a place to love on each other. Justin, Audra, Steve, Lisa, Charles, April, Mike, and Sue—thank you for supporting and cheering this book on in a thousand tangible ways and for encouraging me to write the book even when it was just a small thought.

La Luz Family, hallway, and my students: You guys make my everyday *amazing*. Thank you for taking me under your wing and bringing me into the best tribe ever. I love spending my days with you and doing life with you. I love you all so much it hurts!

Kathryn Haines: Thank you for helping me figure out the world of writing, publishing, and getting this little book baby *out there*! You are a gift from God, and I love that he brought you in my life.

Lysa Terkeurst, Tracie Miles, Proverbs 31 Ministries, and COMPEL: God brought COMPEL into my life at the perfect time. Thank you to the entire team of those who are passionate about equipping writers and giving them the opportunity to take their words to the world. Thank you for giving me the opportunity to write this book. I am *so* thankful for you.

Jason Fikes, Mary Hardegree, Duane Anderson, and the Leafwood Team: You took a chance on me, and I will never stop being thankful for it. I am so grateful for your patience, guidance, and wisdom during this entire process. Thank you for considering every word, for making them better, and remaining passionate about the truth of God being sent to the ends of the earth.

Focus Group: To all the friends and family who saw this book at its barebones: *thank you*. Your feedback, encouragement, and words are scattered throughout every page in this book. Thank you for taking the time to make this book what it is.

To my readers: I am so humbled and honored that you would pick up this book and read it. I hope that someday we can meet, and that I can hear your story of how God freed you from a life of striving for him. I pray for you all the time: that our amazing God would continue setting you more and more free. I am so grateful for you.

ABOUT THE AUTHOR

Kaitlin is a writer, wife, songwriter, women's ministry leader, and second-grade teacher who loves to share about the grace of God through many creative outlets. She is passionate about the next generation of women knowing the truth of the gospel so it may set them free to know Jesus and follow him with their lives. Kaitlin has been featured on Proverbs 31 Ministries' Encouragement for Today and was a contributor in their book *40 Reminders That God Is in Control*. Kaitlin lives with her spunky husband, Lance, in a small town in New Mexico with their two dogs.

Website
If you would like to read more about experiencing God's wild, soul-freeing grace, you can visit Kaitlin's website:

www.kaitlingarrison.com

Social Media
If you would like to connect with Kaitlin on a more regular basis, you can find her here:

Facebook: www.facebook.com/kaitlinngarrison
Instagram: www.instagram.com/kaitlinngarrison